P9-CRX-934

CHICAGO PUBLIC LIBRARY

R03000 51070

DATE DUE

OCT 2 9 2005

DEMCO 38-296

ORIOLE PARK BRANCH
7454 W. BALMORAL
CHICAGO, IL 60656

DISCARD

WOMEN SUFFRAGISTS

DIANA STAR HELMER

Facts On File, Inc.

Women Suffragists

Copyright © 1998 by Diana Star Helmer

All rights reserved. No part of this book may be reproduced or utilized in any form or by any means, electronic or mechanical, including photocopying, recording, or by any information storage or retrieval systems, without permission in writing from the publisher. For information contact:

Facts On File, Inc.
11 Penn Plaza
New York NY 10001

Library of Congress Cataloging-in-Publication Data

Helmer, Diana Star, 1962–
   Women suffragists / Diana Star Helmer.
      p. cm.—(American profiles (Facts on File, Inc.))
   Includes bibliographical references and index.
   Summary: A collective biography of important American women who fought for the female right to vote, including Elizabeth Cady Stanton, Susan B. Anthony, and Sojourner Truth.
   ISBN 0-8160-3579-2
   1. Suffragists—United States—Biography—Juvenile literature.
[1. Suffragist. 2. Women's rights—History. 3. Women—Biography.]
I. Title. II. Series.
JK1898.5.H45   1998
324.62′3′092273—dc21   97-32374
[B]

Facts On File books are available at special discounts when purchased in bulk quantities for businesses, associations, institutions or sales promotions. Please call our Special Sales Department in New York at (212) 967-8800 or (800) 322-8755.

You can find Facts On File on the World Wide Web at http://www.factsonfile.com

Text design by Cathy Rincon
Cover design by Matt Galemmo

Printed in the United States of America

MP FOF 10 9 8 7 6 5 4 3 2

This book is printed on acid-free paper.

R0300051070

Contents

DISCARD

...rk Branch
...4 W. Balmoral Ave.
Chicago, IL 60656

Acknowledgments

Thank you to all of the librarians and historical society members who shared the work they love, especially the reference staff of the Marshalltown Public Library. And to Tom Owens for his help writing the history of my heart.

Introduction

*Oh, all the men make all the laws, which makes the women fret
But wait and see those laws when we at last our suffrage get—*

*Yes, Papa votes but Mama can't—oh, no, not yet, not yet—
And I'll not marry any man till I my suffrage get.
No matter what the others think, I am a suffragette!*

When this song was sung in America of 1912, people understood the words, whether they agreed with them or not. It was true that, ever since the American colonies broke free of England in 1776, men had made the laws. In all but a few remote locations, only men had suffrage: Only men could vote. Even if a woman owned property and paid taxes (which was often legal only if she was single with no male relatives), that woman was not allowed to vote.

Of course, women protested. American government had been founded on the principle that "taxation without representation is tyranny." Paying taxes should entitle taxpayers to a say in how the government spent tax money. Yet in 1912, more than a century after the American Revolution, women still had no say. Laws and customs kept American women from getting the education they wanted and pursuing the careers they chose. Married women could not divorce abusive husbands, get custody of their children, learn about birth control, or inherit family property. Even the money earned by married women belonged legally to their husbands. Many Americans could understand why "laws made women fret," and why a young woman would "not marry any man till I my suffrage get."

THE WIFE AND MOTHER AT A PRIMARY,

THE FATHER STAYS AT HOME, ATTENDING TO THE CHILDREN.

The rowdy voters (top) and unhappy children (bottom) in this 1870 cartoon warn Americans to respect traditional "male" and "female" roles. (Burling Library, Grinnell College)

But others saw danger in women entering politics. Another song had been around since 1867:

> Then mothers, wives, and sisters, I beg you keep your place
> and remain what Nature made you: the helpmeets of our race.
> Let no temptation lead you, nor any wily fox,
> to descend unto the level of the nation's ballotbox.

Listeners knew the age-old meanings here, too. Politics were dirty and corrupt, the song said. Women shouldn't know about such evil, because a woman's job was raising children. Teachers must be innocent and pure and pass that morality on.

Of course, women protested. Amelia Bloomer believed that if the world of politics was "really so bad a place, surely [men] should themselves keep away from it . . . I hold that any place that is too corrupt for a woman to go is too corrupt for a man to go." Ten years after this song appeared, Carrie Chapman Catt wondered, "How is it possible that a woman who is unfit to vote should be the mother of, and bring up, a man who is?"

Some women wanted to have a say in government and be more active outside the home. Other women did not. But only men could change the laws. More often than not, men listened to the women who did not want to change. Not changing was easy—and safe. After all, if women changed, men would have to change, too. "[Men] have frightened themselves with the belief . . . that men would have to turn housekeepers and nursemaids" if women did "manly" things like voting, Bloomer said.

Many American men—and women—didn't like the thought of old roles changing. They feared losing their own, familiar identities. Yet most of the suffragists in this book did not want to change women's roles entirely. Seven of the ten were married, and four combined their careers with raising families. Two who didn't have children raised those belonging to others.

Suffragists just wanted choices. "Do not tell us before we are born even that our province is to cook dinners, darn stockings and sew on buttons," Lucy Stone told an 1855 audience. "I have confidence in [God] to believe that, when He gives us the capacity to do anything, He does not make a blunder. Leave women, then, to find their sphere."

Every suffragist had a different sphere, different reasons for dedicating herself to the cause. Elizabeth Cady Stanton wanted women to be valued. Susan B. Anthony wanted women to be able to protect themselves from social evils, like alcohol. Sojourner Truth wanted women to know what true freedom was. Lucy Stone wanted equal education. Victoria Woodhull wanted financial independence. Amelia Bloomer wanted women to believe that their well-being was more important than custom. Mary Church Terrell wanted women of color to be accepted as able citizens. Carrie Chapman Catt wanted women to understand politics. And Alice Paul and Jeanette Rankin wanted women—one half of the human race—to be able to work for peace. Each woman came to realize that her goal would not, could not, come true, if women had no voice. Suffrage—the vote—was that voice.

Tradition was an obstacle all suffragists had to hurdle. Each of these suffragists also had personal challenges to overcome. Stanton's was her many children. Terrell described the difficulties of being "a colored woman in a white world." Health affected many of the women: Lucy Stone, Amelia Bloomer, and Carrie Chapman Catt suffered from migraine headaches.

Personalities may have been defined by health problems that were untreatable, even unnamed, at the time. Victoria Woodhull's erratic behavior, courageously outspoken one moment, unwisely vindictive the next, earned her the nickname "Mrs. Satan," hinting at evil or insanity. Current medical knowledge suggests that some of Woodhull's struggles may have been signs of mental illness that is treatable today but wasn't during her life. Her actions are often hard to understand but should not be ignored because of that. Woodhull dared to do, when few women dared even talk. "If I do nothing else," she said, "I know that I have awakened investigation . . . If all I have said is error; if the truth lies in altogether different directions from those in which I point, out of the discussion now going on the truth will be evolved."

Woodhull knew that truth doesn't always lie in one direction but in a combination of paths. Most destinations are reached by taking first one path, then another and another. The paths of these biographies combine to tell the story of America's early women's rights movement.

Though not born first, Elizabeth Cady Stanton began the unified effort for women's votes in 1848. Because Stanton worked so closely with Susan B. Anthony, their stories needed to be together. The later stories of Alice Paul and Carrie Chapman Catt were inseparable, too, but for the opposite reason: Public response to Paul's 1917 protests forced President Woodrow Wilson to change his stand on woman suffrage. Rather than acknowledge Paul's influence, however, he endorsed the more conservative Catt. Between these four biographies, other stories are placed in chronology of the subject's most active years. Lucy Stone and Sojourner Truth were two early activists whose work was shaped by the Civil War. Amelia Bloomer was also part of those vigorous years, but her postwar work was halted by that of Victoria Woodhull. Mary Church Terrell, born just as African Americans were given freedom, showed the potential of a postslavery world. And, as Stanton seemed to begin women's odyssey toward equality, Jeannette Rankin seemed to complete it. Rankin was the first woman elected to the U.S. Congress, a direct result of women's votes.

American women's unified efforts to be a part of democracy began in 1848, with Elizabeth Cady Stanton's women's rights convention. Yet 21 years went by before Wyoming territory gave its women the vote. Utah territory followed in 1870. Twenty more years passed before Wyoming became a state in 1890, and Wyoming women became the first in the union to vote. By 1900, the states of Utah, Colorado, and Idaho had woman suffrage, too.

Then, for 12 years, nothing. Suffragists traveled the country trying to convince men to vote for women's right to vote. Carriages were uncomfortable, slow, and inconvenient. So were boats and steam-engine trains. Suffragists got sick from bad water or local viruses. They didn't talk about their frustrations to men—men had to be wooed, coddled, and coaxed into granting women the vote.

In 1970, this U.S. postage stamp celebrated 50 years of woman suffrage, showing the parade pickets that led to modern women's votes.
(U.S. Postal Service. Reproduced with permission.)

Reforms "move invariably onward in waves of success followed by inevitable reaction," said suffragist Carrie Chapman Catt. Not until 1912 did women make any further progress on U.S. suffrage. That year, Arizona, Kansas, and Oregon granted women the right to vote. Montana and Nevada followed in 1914. In 1917, North Dakota, Ohio, Indiana, Rhode Island, Nebraska, Michigan, New York, and Arkansas became a "wave of success" for woman suffrage. Finally, in 1920, 36 states ratified the 19th Amendment to the U.S. Constitution: "The right of the citizens of the United States to vote shall not be denied or abridged by the United States or by any state on account of sex." Woman suffrage was now a legal fact.

But the accompanying joy was followed by the "inevitable reaction." "After the passing of the 19th Amendment," Catt said, "I discovered that men who had been most enthusiastic in the campaign to give the vote to women were shocked and grieved at the idea of [a] woman's entering into politics or holding office. You see, their minds had changed on one point only. More alterations had to be made."

One of the alterations that needed to be made was history. History reflects the attitudes of historians. Historians who had studied histories of men wrote more histories of men. Teachers taught what they had learned: the histories of men. So, even though some women wrote women's histories, they seldom received much attention.

Of course, women's histories also reflect the attitudes of their tellers. In their six-volume *History of Woman Suffrage*, Elizabeth Cady Stanton and Susan B. Anthony present a story of cooperation under the leadership of the National American Woman Suffrage Association (NAWSA). They refused to include some stories, like Amelia Bloomer's account of the rocky Iowa campaign. Carrie Chapman Catt wrote a different, angry history, accusing businessmen and politicians of delaying woman suffrage with corruption and malice.

Stanton and Anthony's less controversial version has had the greatest effect on historians. Yet their retelling often downplayed suffragists outside the NAWSA circle. Lucy Stone's American Woman Suffrage Association kept suffragists active in the late 1800s when members fled from the unsettled NAWSA. Alice Paul broke from NAWSA in 1914 and began pressur ing the government with parades, hunger strikes, and the burning of presidential speeches. NAWSA insisted these "militant" tactics damaged the cause. But

Senator John Warner (R-Virginia) speaks at the unveiling and rededication of the "Mothers of Suffrage" statue, June 26, 1997. Suffrage leader Alice Paul originally dedicated the tribute to suffrage pioneers Elizabeth Cady Stanton, Lucretia Mott, and Susan B. Anthony on February 15, 1921, the 100th anniversary of Anthony's birth. But the Joint Library Committee claimed that the Capitol had "enough statues" without sculptor Adelaide Johnson's 8-ton monument. For almost 75 years, the work remained undiscovered or unknown to many Capitol visitors. The rededication placed the memorial in the Capitol rotunda's Hall of Statues. (Photo courtesy of office of Senator John Warner)

Paul's protests closely precipitated changes in the president's suffrage policy. Her agenda didn't hurt, and probably, it helped.

Such disagreements made the struggle for suffrage more difficult. And even success didn't unify the women who had pressed for one goal. Alice Paul went on to lobby for the addition of the Equal Rights Amendment to the U.S. Constitution: "Equality of rights . . . shall not be denied . . . on account of sex." But Catt believed that equal rights would mean starting from scratch, doing away with protective laws that women had struggled for. "Prejudices will not melt away because the Constitution declares equal rights," Catt said.

Perhaps this lack of unity is really a sign of success. The fight for suffrage was a struggle to allow women to use their voices. Now it's up to every woman to find her voice.

Eng^d by H B Hall Jr N Y

ELIZABETH CADY STANTON

(1815–1902)

Elizabeth Cady had finally graduated and was home from school. She would probably stay there the rest of her life, unless she married. But Cady wasn't one to just sit around, waiting for something to happen. She joined groups, like the Presbyterian Girls' Club, which decided to help a young man from the area become a minister. Cady helped raise money for his schooling. She helped get a fine suit of clothes for him to preach in after he graduated. The Girls' Club even arranged for him to preach his very first sermon from their church pulpit. Of course, Cady and her friends came to hear.

Their beneficiary, their special project, their preacher began his sermon. He based his words on the Bible verse, "I suffer not a woman to teach, nor to usurp authority over the man, but to be in silence."

Opposite: *Elizabeth Cady Stanton called the first-ever woman's rights convention in 1848. Many people thought women needed just a few specific rights, such as property or child custody. Stanton wanted complete equal rights, including the right to vote.*
(Burling Library, Grinnell College)

Cady would suffer not to listen to this. She walked out while he was talking, aware of the eyes upon her.

Elizabeth Cady was born on November 12, 1815, in Johnstown, New York. Her mother, Margaret Livingston Cady, was the daughter of a Revolutionary War hero. She inherited a commanding attitude. Cady's father, Daniel, was a well-to-do lawyer and congressman before he became a circuit court judge. Elizabeth was born the middle of ten children, five girls and five boys, but every boy died of illness. Elizabeth never forgot Judge Cady's words soon after one son's death: "Oh, my daughter, I wish you were a boy."

Those words convinced Elizabeth to study subjects reserved for boys, such as Greek and horseback riding. Studying law in her father's office, she saw why he wished for boys. A woman came to Judge Cady trying to get her farm back. When she'd married, the law had given it to her husband. Upon his death, the farm legally belonged to her irresponsible son. But Judge Cady was powerless to help her. American law gave women no rights, and neither could Judge Cady.

He did give his daughter an education. Elizabeth Cady graduated from Johnstown Academy and Emma Willard's Female Seminary in Troy, New York. But there wasn't much for a respectable, well-off young woman to do after that. Cady spent a lot of time in Peterboro with her cousin Gerrit Smith's family. Smith's house was a station on the Underground Railroad, a network of houses where runaway slaves hid and rested before moving on. There, Cady met other reformers who wanted to stop slavery, abolitionists like the dynamic Henry Stanton.

Unlike Cady's father, Stanton didn't stop at obeying the law. He wanted to change the law. When Stanton proposed marriage to Cady, she accepted right away, though she knew her father would object.

Cady and Stanton eloped. There wasn't much time for preparation, anyway. They wanted to combine their honeymoon trip with a world antislavery convention in London. Henry Stanton was a delegate. Rushing to arrive on time, Cady still made sure that the wedding vows did not ask her to "obey" her husband. Henry Stanton, charmed by his petite, vivacious bride, did not protest. Yet before the trip was over, his pleas for more traditional behavior from Elizabeth Cady Stanton proved he wasn't ready for a wife who made her own rules.

Henry Stanton wanted a political career. The new Mrs. Stanton didn't seem to understand that part of politics was not offending others. Instead of befriending the wives of his fellow party members, she became fast friends with Lucretia Mott, an outspoken Quaker delegate. The Quakers were a Christian sect that rejected ceremonies such as weddings and funerals and sacraments such as communion and opposed war. Like other Quakers of her time, Lucretia Mott lived and dressed simply, to better search for her "inner light." Other religions doubted if women had souls. But Quakers encouraged women to speak their mind. Mott protested when Englishmen disregarded female delegates to the antislavery convention. Elizabeth Stanton was delighted when her husband spoke for the women. But when it came time to vote, he voted with his party—against letting women participate. After all, he explained, it was hard enough to get people to support new rights for blacks, without asking them to give new rights to women, too.

After the convention, the Stantons took a honeymoon tour of Europe that allowed Henry some speaking engagements. But Elizabeth chose to stay in Dublin for one month without Henry because she couldn't stop arguing "the woman question" with his escorts.

Back in the United States, Henry Stanton tried a number of professions: lawyer, journalist, lecturer, elected official. Elizabeth Cady Stanton gave birth to her first child in 1842. She had three boys by the end of 1846. Two more boys and two girls would arrive by 1859, totaling seven children over 17 years.

In those early years, Stanton loved showing off her "executive ability." Raising children and running her own home was fun in Boston, where she could hire domestic help and take part in rousing reform groups. But by 1847, money ran low. Judge Cady offered the young couple a country house in Seneca Falls. It was an ideal solution for Henry Stanton, who traveled for his work anyway. But far from the clubs and causes of Boston, Elizabeth Cady Stanton felt alone.

In 1848, a letter arrived with news of Lucretia Mott. Stanton and Mott had corresponded since meeting in London in 1840. Mott was

Whatever is done to lift woman to her true position will help to usher in a new day of peace and perfection for the race.

—Elizabeth Cady Stanton

coming to visit her sister in Seneca Falls, so now they could meet again. A mutual friend invited Stanton and Mott to a sociable gathering of five women reformers. Only Stanton wasn't Quaker. But she was the youngest, and her frustrations with womanhood were the most raw.

Stanton's words poured out in "a torrent of my long-accumulated discontent" that day. She had everything that people said a woman needed to be happy, but her life was unfulfilling. Housework was endless, and she had no help. She was lucky that childbirth was easy for her, but raising those children never stopped, and new babies just kept coming. But the worst was Stanton's "mental hunger." Her work was drudgery, with no true challenges. She saw no adults, only her children. Their happy chatter cheered her heart, but didn't inspire her mind.

Glances and nods of understanding echoed from face to face. The others had experienced the same dead ends. They knew Stanton's yearnings. Most women did. Something ought to be done, they agreed. And when something needed doing in mid-19th century America, reformers called a convention. These women had all attended conventions for abolition and temperance. They would call a convention to discuss women's rights—the right to do more than care for homes, the right to be educated so they'd have other choices, the right to make choices without a husband's or a father's approval. And with the famous Lucretia Mott in their midst, this was the perfect time. How long Mott would stay was uncertain, so the sooner the meeting, the better.

The women began planning right away. They picked a location, Seneca Falls' liberal Methodist church. They reserved the spot and put an announcement in the next day's newspaper. The five women had less than a week to plan a two-day convention. Stanton plunged into writing the group's statement of purpose. After all, her frustration had sparked the whole project.

She based her words on the Declaration of Independence. Though the document was so new that Stanton's grandparents could recall when it was written, it was already almost sacred to Americans. If they'd only remember how shocking that declaration had been at first, Stanton's new words might not seem quite so radical.

"When in the course of human events . . ." Stanton began her declaration the same way the original began. She went on, "The history of mankind is a history of repeated injuries . . . on the part of man toward woman, having in direct object the establishment of an absolute tyranny over her. To prove this, let facts be submitted to a candid world.

"He has never permitted her to exercise her inalienable right to the elective franchise."

Even Lucretia Mott protested. The idea of women voting was "ridiculous," she said. Stanton should focus on other "facts," such as man "monopoliz[ing] nearly all the profitable employments" or denying women "the facilities for a thorough education" or "giving to the world a different set of moral codes for men and women, by which moral delinquencies which exclude women from society, are not only tolerated, but deemed of little account in man."

Stanton heard few complaints about these unladylike comments on sex. But at the planning meetings and the convention, the idea of women voting incited protest, discussion, and dissent. To Stanton, voting was the one right that would help women obtain all others, the right that would remove women from a separate class and acknowledge them as leaders of humanity. She would not take out the demand.

Wednesday, July 19, 1848, was hot in Seneca Falls. Stanton had children to feed and dress before 10 A.M. and a visiting sister to worry about. Her husband had left town in a snit over the thought of women voting, and Stanton knew her coplanners still objected, too. Worse, Stanton was scheduled to speak

T*he trouble was not in what I said, but that I said it too soon, and before the people were ready to hear it. It may be, however, that I helped them to get ready; who knows?*

—Elizabeth Cady Stanton

but had never done so in front of a crowd. There might not be a crowd, anyway. There had been time for only one notice in the papers, and meeting on a weekday would probably keep poor young working women away. So Stanton had no specific focus for her fears until she rounded the corner to the church and saw the people. Three hundred people stood outside because the church door was locked. And Stanton didn't have a key.

Her visiting sister, however, had an 11-year-old son. He was hoisted through a window to open the door from the other side.

For Lucretia Mott and her husband, James, and other Quakers, the convention was much like others they'd attended. Quaker women spoke and preached and lectured in public as men did. But non-Quakers in the audience had rarely seen women address and interact in a group, especially a so-called promiscuous crowd of both genders. Stanton herself, according to the Seneca Falls *Courier*, barely spoke above a whisper at first. But before she finished reading her declaration, her voice took on the power of her words.

During the next two mornings proposals were introduced for the betterment of women. The afternoons were filled debating those ideas. Evenings featured lectures by Lucretia Mott, with comments and discussion by others, including Stanton and famed abolitionist Frederick Douglass. Before the convention ended, Stanton's Declaration of Sentiments was signed by 100 men and women, twice as many women as men.

But the convention wasn't really over. Two weeks later, the Seneca County *Courier* reprinted the Declaration of Sentiments. When New York newspapers picked up the story, the nationwide controversy over woman suffrage began. Just at that time, women who had attended the meeting in Seneca Falls staged their own convention in Rochester. Other conventions followed, sometimes with Stanton on hand, sometimes with just her ideas. But those ideas, well written and legally sound, took on a life of their own.

Stanton spoke at nearby conventions when she could. She began hosting "conversations" in Seneca Falls where reformers met and discussed women's rights. She persuaded Amelia Bloomer, the editor of a local temperance paper, to publish articles Stanton wrote linking temperance and women's rights. And there were plenty of other newspapers to write to. Whenever Stanton heard of an editor who made sarcastic remarks about a women's rights convention, she replied in a letter to the editor.

The children and housework still took more time than Stanton liked, but at least she had mental diversions now. And housework was easier, thanks to Stanton's cousin, Libby Smith Miller. She'd come to visit wearing an incredible new dress, loose fitting and knee length, with trousers underneath. Stanton had trouble working in the long, tight dresses considered "proper" for women. She wanted freedom for women, and these wonderful short skirts let her carry a baby and a candle upstairs, without holding onto long skirts. Inspired with physical freedom, Stanton even cut off her cascading curls, though most women never cut their hair. Her father, husband, and sons were mortified. But Stanton needed the advantage of free movement if she were to be responsible for a house and family that now had four boys, with a new baby on the way.

Different advantages came her way in 1851, when Stanton met Susan B. Anthony. They were friends for the rest of Stanton's life. Stanton met another important woman that year, too. Amelia Willard, Stanton said, was "one of the best gifts of the gods . . . a good, faithful housekeeper . . . But for this noble, self-sacrificing woman, much of my public work would have been quite impossible." Willard worked for the Stantons for 31 years.

Willard's role was that of the traditional wife. But it was Anthony about whom Stanton wrote, "So entirely one are we . . . To the world we always seem to agree and uniformly reflect each other. Like husband and wife . . ."

Together, they planned conventions, lecture tours, speeches, editorials, and protests. Stanton, still frequently confined with pregnancies, counted on Anthony's organizational and recruiting skills. Anthony depended on Stanton's words. "How I wish I had Mrs. Stanton here," Anthony once wrote, "and I could galvanize her to make beautiful my crude glimmering of ideas."

Anthony often wrote half-funny, half-serious letters, alternately begging for help or scolding Stanton to action. Stanton jokingly called her friend a "tyrant," but admitted "I do believe that I have developed into much more of a woman under her jurisdictions, fed on statute laws and constitutional amendments, than if left to myself . . ."

Even with Amelia Willard's help, the seven Stanton children required another adult on hand if their mother was to do other work. Anthony often stayed with the Stantons, watching the children while hatching political ideas with their mother. Anthony was so much a part of the household that the children called her "Aunt Susan."

Together Stanton and Anthony petitioned and lobbied for married women's rights in New York State, including fairer divorce laws. They prepared an address on women's rights for Stanton to deliver in 1854 to the New York state legislature. Only Anthony came to see Stanton give her first speech to an official government assembly. Stanton's husband and father disapproved of women putting themselves on public display. But when the last of Stanton's children were born and she began her speaking career in 1860, Henry Stanton didn't object to the lecture money she contributed to their children's college funds.

The Civil War interrupted Stanton's long-awaited freedom. In a country torn apart by slavery, women's rights seemed beside the point. Stanton and Anthony would have to wait for listeners. In the meantime, they both believed in freedom for blacks, and neither woman was the sort to sit around and wait for things to happen. They formed the Women's Loyal League in 1863 to support the Republican party's antislavery work. After the war, they thought, women's loyalty would be rewarded with votes.

But when the war ended in 1865, politicians realized that the reality of freeing the slaves was going to change American life. The idea of "Negro rights" was new and strange enough for Americans to get used to without adjusting to new roles for women. The Republicans asked women to wait for the vote. The public might not give the freed slaves their rights if women changed their roles, too, Republicans said. They urged Stanton and her colleagues to support the 14th Amendment, which was meant to give rights to freed slaves. But the amendment promised those rights specifically to males. Before the 14th Amendment, only state and local decrees had denied women's rights. The new amendment made women's voicelessness a matter of national policy.

Stanton was furious. Well, they could pass laws forbidding her to vote, but they hadn't passed any laws forbidding her to run for office.

In 1866, Elizabeth Cady Stanton ran for Congress from the eighth district of New York. She bragged for years about the 24 votes she received. That same year, she, Anthony, and others formed the American Equal Rights Association (AERA), a group dedicated to acquiring the vote for both women and blacks.

She and Anthony went to Kansas in 1867, campaigning for equal rights. An upcoming public vote there would decide if women, blacks, or both would be enfranchised. Stanton was not disappointed in her long-awaited adventures "in the field." The pioneer life in Kansas was harsh—so was the fight by liquor interests that opposed woman suffrage, thinking women's votes would ban alcohol. The Kansas campaign failed. But in Kansas, Stanton and Anthony met a rich man who thought women's rights needed a newspaper—and he was willing to put his money where his mouth was. Stanton was thrilled. A paper of her own, to say all the things she wanted to say!

The Revolution debuted in January 1868, with Anthony as publisher and Stanton as editor. Stanton wrote article after article criticizing politicians and other organizations—including Christian churches—for mistreating women and minorities. She wasn't shy about expressing her beliefs. Stanton had nothing to lose. Her father had already threatened to disown her. Her husband thought she'd ruined his career. Other members of the AERA thought Stanton's attacks on the church had nothing to do with women's votes. But Stanton thought everything had to do with women. Education, employment practices, science, medicine, laws, and religion all affected what people thought about women. Public opinion determined whether women would be allowed to vote.

Surely a government of the most virtuous, educated men and women would better represent the whole, and protect the interests of all than could the representation of either sex alone.

—Elizabeth Cady Stanton

Struggling with allies was even worse than struggling with enemies. Stanton and Anthony finally broke away from the AERA in 1869. They formed their own group, the National Woman Suffrage Association (NWSA). Stanton was elected the group's first president. She urged the small membership to work for an amendment to the U.S. Constitution that would guarantee women the right to vote. For 20 years, they fought with petitions and protests, with speeches and impatience, with Stanton either leading the group or not far down the ranks. Stanton and Anthony recorded the history of the struggle in the *History of Woman Suffrage.* The first of six volumes was published in 1881.

Stanton was 75 years old when her daughter finally persuaded her to rejoin the suffragists from the AERA. Their reunited organization, the National American Woman Suffrage Association (NAWSA), elected Stanton as its first president.

When Stanton was 80, she almost split the group again by writing *The Woman's Bible.* In it, Stanton and other women examined biblical texts, not as sacred documents, but as words written down, interpreted, and passed down by men. Stanton believed that "Religious superstitions of women perpetuate their bondage more than all other adverse influences . . ." Naturally, referring to Christian practices as "superstitions" did not please the religious establishment. Even Anthony felt such philosophies distracted people from the true cause: woman suffrage. "I get more radical as I grow older," Stanton sighed, "while [Susan] seems to get more conservative."

Yet the two women "jogged along pretty well," Stanton wrote, with "few ripples on the surface." She told her friend, "You are intertwined with much of my happy and eventful past, and all my future plans are based on you as a coadjutor."

When Stanton's next book, her memoir, was published in 1898, it was dedicated "To Susan B. Anthony, my steadfast friend for half a century." Stanton devoted two chapters to Anthony, plus many other references. Husband Henry Stanton is rarely mentioned. The Stantons had grown apart during their marriage. Henry's death in 1887 would not be half so hard on his wife as her death was on Susan B. Anthony.

In New York's Woodlawn Cemetery, Stanton's huge graveside monument spells out her many achievements for women's rights. (Courtesy of Jim Tipton/Find-A-Grave web page)

Elizabeth Cady Stanton died in her New York home on October 26, 1902. She had already become what she is today, a symbol of feminism. Then, as now, the word *feminism* is often misused to mean "antimale." But Stanton, a devoted mother of five sons, a faithful (though not obedient) wife and daughter, was never antimale. The start of the entire movement proves that.

The door to the church where Stanton held her historic first Woman's Rights Convention was locked. She asked her nephew to climb in a window. Because a boy respected the women who helped and cared for him, he took an unusual path. He opened the door from his side so that women could come in, too.

To Stanton, feminism was as simple as that. Women and men share this world. If all people are allowed to use their capabilities, the world can truly prosper. "Resolved," Stanton finished her Declaration of Sentiments, "that the speedy success of our cause depends upon the zealous and untiring efforts of both men and women. . . ."

Chronology

NOVEMBER 12, 1815	Elizabeth Cady born in Johnstown, New York
1832	graduates from Emma Willard Female Seminary in Troy, New York
1840	marries Henry Brewster Stanton; attends world antislavery convention in London
1848	organizes Woman's Rights Convention in Seneca Falls; writes the "Declaration of Sentiments" asking for woman suffrage
1851	meets Susan B. Anthony
1854	addresses New York legislature
1860	embarks upon cross-country speaking career
1863	forms Women's Loyal League with Anthony

1866	runs for New York seat in Congress; co-founds the American Equal Rights Association
1868	becomes editor and writer for *The Revolution*
1869	National Woman Suffrage Association (NWSA) founded; Stanton elected first president
1881	cowrites and publishes volume I of the *History of Woman Suffrage*
1887	Henry Stanton dies
1890	National American Woman Suffrage Association (NAWSA) formed; Stanton elected president
1895	publishes first installment of *The Woman's Bible*
1898	memoir *Eighty Years and More* is published
OCTOBER 26, 1902	Elizabeth Cady Stanton dies in New York City

Further Reading

Cullen-Dupont, Kathryn. *Elizabeth Cady Stanton & Women's Liberty.* New York: Facts On File, 1992. A biography aimed at young adults.

Fritz, Jean. *You Want Women to Vote, Lizzie Stanton?* New York: G.P. Putnam's Sons, 1995. A brief, lively biography for young readers.

Johnston, Norma. *Remember the Ladies: The First Women's Rights Convention.* New York: Scholastic, 1995. Well-documented account of the beginnings of the women's rights movement for young readers.

Rossi, Alice S., editor. *The Feminist Papers: From Adams to Beauvoir.* New York: Columbia University Press, 1973. Actual historical documents of the women's rights movement include Stanton's *Introduction to the Woman's Bible,* an essay on motherhood, and the Declaration of Sentiments. Contains an essay on Stanton and Anthony's friendship, documented with letters. Stanton's writings are often formal and challenging in style. Rossi's editorials are accessible to young adult readers.

Stanton, Elizabeth Cady. *Eighty Years and More.* Boston: Northeastern University Press, 1993 (reprinted from 1898 original). Stanton's reminiscences are sometimes too chatty, filled with details but not dates. She included such facts in four volumes of the *History of Woman Suffrage.*

SUSAN B. ANTHONY

(1820–1906)

No matter what 17-year-old Susan B. Anthony did, she could not seem to please the headmistress. Anthony was trying. She knew her father was spending money he didn't have to send her and her sister to this rare, female boarding school. Arithmetic, algebra, literature, chemistry, philosophy, physiology, and bookkeeping weren't so bad. Unfortunately, the subject that got "particular attention" at Deborah Moulson's Female Seminary was "the inculcation of the principles of Humility, Morality and love of Virtue."

That meant doing tasks thoroughly and according to the rules. But Anthony got so excited writing a paper, she forgot to put dots over her i's. She focused so intensely on dusting cobwebs from the ceiling that she tripped over a piece of furniture and broke it. She believed she was "guilty of much levity and nonsensical conversation," and "thoughts . . . which should have been far distant" from her mind. Her sister Guelma had no such troubles. "Thy sister Guelma does the best she is capable of, but thou dost not," Deborah Moulson sniffed. "Thou hast greater abilities, and I demand of thee the best of thy capacity."

Susan B. Anthony was famous, not only for her persuasive logic, but for the plain clothes and stern expressions that symbolized her tenacity. (Burling Library, Grinnell College)

Anthony had no one she could tell her troubles to. Moulson read any letters students wrote to their parents. "Perhaps the reason I cannot see my own defects is because my heart is hardened," Anthony wrote in her diary. She dreamed at night about improving. Sixty years later, the thought of that school would still make Anthony "turn cold and sick at heart."

Susan Brownell Anthony was born on February 15, 1820, in Adams, Massachusetts. Her father, Daniel Anthony, was a cotton mill owner who treated his employees like members of his family.

Workers had their own housing with garden plots. Their children studied with the Anthony children's private teacher. In the evenings, mill workers got schooling, too. Susan, the second of seven children, grew up helping her mother and sisters cook for many mouths. Susan's music-loving mother, Lucy Read Anthony, had adopted her husband's Quaker ways, avoiding wine and song. But Susan's father let non-Quaker workers dance after hours in his building. If young folks didn't dance there, he reasoned, they'd go to a tavern, which was worse. But his logic wasn't good enough for the church, and Daniel Anthony was "disowned."

Quaker beliefs continued to shape his life, however, and they shaped Susan's. She learned at a young age to be proud of hard work. Her father, like some other Quakers but unlike many men of his day, believed all young people should learn to earn a living. He sent Susan and her older sister to learn teaching at Deborah Moulson's expensive Quaker girls' school in 1837. But that year, the economy plummeted. By 1838, Daniel Anthony was forced to bring his daughters home. Susan didn't mind. In almost two years, she'd never stopped being homesick.

For the next 10 years, Susan B. Anthony taught in various schools, coming home on break whenever she could. In 1845, her parents moved to a farm in Rochester. Antislavery Quakers met there almost every Sunday, sometimes joined by famous activists like Frederick Douglass and William Lloyd Garrison. Two of Anthony's brothers quit the farm for antislavery activism. Anthony began to feel restless, too. A job promotion distracted her, for a while. At age 26, she headed the girls' department at Canajoharie Academy, earning $110 a year. But by 1848, Anthony confessed in a letter home, "I have to manufacture the interest duty compels me to exhibit." She joined a local women's group, the Daughters of Temperance. Anthony's father had taught what this group practiced, that stronger liquor laws made stronger families. Anthony didn't have to "manufacture interest" here.

She gave up teaching. "Woman must take to her soul a purpose and then make circumstances conform to this purpose," Anthony said a few years later, "instead of forever singing the refrain, 'if and if and if.'" Anthony moved to Rochester in 1849, where she was elected president of the local Daughters of Temperance. Her family

> **W**_hoever controls_
> _work and wages,_
> _controls morals._
>
> —Susan B. Anthony

helped and encouraged all her work, as they always would. And, being Anthonys, they introduced her to other causes. Daniel, Lucy, and sister Mary had attended an 1848 woman's rights convention in Rochester and been electrified by the ideas of young Elizabeth Cady Stanton. They'd actually signed Stanton's radical Declaration of Sentiments, a document demanding equal rights for women, including the right to vote. Even Daniel had signed, the same man who'd once told Susan that their best mill worker couldn't be an overseer because she was a woman.

Susan Anthony still remembered those words. But she decided that liquor was a more immediate problem. She had seen the results of alcoholism in other families. She knew temperance could change people's lives.

In 1853, Anthony went as a delegate to the state convention of the Sons of Temperance in Albany. When she rose to speak on a motion, Anthony was silenced with the words, "The sisters were not invited here to speak, but to listen and learn." Anthony left the hall, followed by a few other women.

Soon after that infuriating temperance convention, Anthony attended the 1853 state teacher's convention. Again, her wish to speak caused an uproar. Anthony was finally allowed to say why she thought teachers were not well respected. Teaching was one of the few jobs open to both genders, she pointed out. Quite likely, the public believed that any job a woman could do was unimportant. "Would you exalt your profession," Anthony told the men, "exalt those who labor with you . . . increase the salaries of the women engaged in the noble work of educating our future presidents, senators and congressmen."

No matter what Anthony tried, her work boomeranged back to the question of gender. As a woman without rights, Anthony could not "take to her soul a purpose."

Her purpose became women's rights. She would spend her life making "circumstances conform to this purpose."

She began with an 1853 campaign for women's property rights in New York State. Anthony spoke at meetings, collected petitions, and lobbied the state legislature. More and more, she asked for help from Elizabeth Cady Stanton. They'd met by chance on a street corner two years before, and Anthony promptly shared her family's high opinion of Stanton. The two made an ideal team. Staying at Stanton's home, Anthony "stirred the pudding" so Stanton could write speeches. Stanton once said, "In writing, we did better work together than either could alone. . . . She supplied the facts and statistics, I the philosophy and rhetoric. . . ." Then Anthony studied the written pages so she could deliver the speech. "Our work is one," Stanton told Anthony, "we are one in aim and sympathy and we should be together." Anthony even considered the Stanton children "my children."

Anthony's eye for detail and organization focused Stanton's fluid words. Their collaborations were filled with quotes from great minds and examples proving their theories. To Anthony and Stanton, women's rights was a question of logic. But to others, it was a question of religion. Anthony wryly acknowledged that many people took the Christian Bible so literally they thought "St. Paul would feel badly about it" if women had equal rights. Crowds threw things, shouted insults, threatened Anthony with weapons, burned her image in effigy, and still Anthony kept speaking. Only one criticism was too much for her.

Anthony believed women should not wear restrictive, unhealthy clothes just because they were "proper" and fashionable. She followed Stanton's lead, donning the short "Bloomer" dress and cutting her hair short. But Anthony, used to modest Quaker clothes, felt garish and gaudy. Audiences could tell. They heckled her without mercy. Stanton begged her friend to go back to regular clothes and save her energy for greater fights. Finally, Anthony agreed.

Back in the plain clothes that became her trademark, Anthony continued her crusades. Her primary goal was woman suffrage, because "there was no true freedom for Woman without the possession of all her property rights, and . . . these rights could be obtained through legislation only," Anthony wrote in her diary in 1853. "[T]he sooner the demand was made of the legislature, the sooner would we be likely to obtain them."

After meeting in 1851, Anthony (standing) and Elizabeth Cady Stanton became friends and comrades for 50 years. Their pose here symbolizes their roles: The active Anthony often caried out the plans they created together. (Smithsonian Institution)

In 1854, Anthony began a New York campaign for woman suffrage, speaking and traveling alone. But her work wasn't solitary. She and Stanton wrote letters faithfully to each other throughout their lives. Anthony often visited Stanton, and they planned conventions that brought suffragists together. Anthony was inspired by women who thought as she did, like Lucy Stone and Antoinette Brown—until Stone and Brown married the Blackwell brothers. In 1857, Anthony canceled her National Woman's Rights Convention, writing: "I feel discouraged when I think of holding a Convention without Lucy or Antoinette—but they are bound to give themselves over to the ineffable joys of Maternity." In 1858, she wrote to Antoinette Brown: "Now, Nettie, not another baby is my peremptory command," adding, "I am provoked at Lucy . . . I do feel it is so foolish for her to put herself in the position of maid of all work and baby tender. . . ."

Anthony made the choice never to marry. "I would not consent that the man I loved . . . should unite his destinies in marriage with a political slave and pariah." Yet, despite her grumbling, Anthony fought for married women's rights. In 1860, largely as the result of her efforts, the New York State Married Women's Property Bill became law, allowing married women to own property, keep their own wages, and have custody of their children.

Anthony's views on marriage were considered extreme, and so were her views on slavery. Her message, "No Union With Slaveholders," dared Southern states to either end slavery or secede, leave the United States and form a separate, slaveholding government. In 1860, some Southern states took the dare, and the Civil War divided America. Anthony struggled to keep women's rights in people's minds. She and Stanton formed the Women's Loyal League in 1863 to petition for the 13th Amendment outlawing slavery. The league reminded voters that blacks needed more than freedom. Blacks needed citizenship and suffrage—and so did women.

Anthony supported the Republican party's 13th Amendment, believing the party would return the favor and en-

Independence is happiness.

—Susan B. Anthony

dorse woman suffrage. But after the 13th Amendment freed the slaves, the proposed 14th Amendment stated outright that only American males could vote. Anthony had been betrayed.

In 1866, Anthony, Stanton, Stone, and others founded the American Equal Rights Association (AERA). For two long years they toured and talked, trying to keep voters from ratifying the hated 14th Amendment. In 1867, Kansas became a battlefield when both woman and black suffrage came up for voter referendums.

Anthony was used to hard campaigns. She was even used to losing battles. She wasn't used to heroes, and there never was a hero quite like George Francis Train. Train was a millionaire who had been invited to speak for suffrage in Kansas. He sang, he wore frills and fancy boots, he waved his purple-gloved hands as he spoke. When people came to see the show, Train let them know that "every man in Kansas who throws a vote for the Negro and not for women has insulted his mother, his daugther, his sister, and his wife!"

Anthony and Train began traveling together. After all, two speakers would make it doubly worth a listener's time to come, especially when the speakers were so different. They both wanted woman suffrage, but unlike Anthony, Train was funny and flamboyant—and antiblack. Anthony was uncertain about the alliance, but she remembered that the 14th Amendment was forcing a choice between blacks and women. Anthony chose women.

One evening during his lecture, Train announced that Anthony was about to found a newspaper called *The Revolution*. Its message, he said, was "Men, their rights, and nothing more; women, their rights, and nothing less." Anthony was astonished, but since Train was putting up all the money, she certainly didn't object. Anthony's organizational skills made her the perfect publisher. Her unmarried life left her free to keep the strict schedule publishing demanded. Stanton, still caring for seven children, snatched moments here and there to write. Their *Revolution* advocated eight-hour workdays, equal pay for equal work, buying American-made goods, abolishing standing armies, universal education, and organized labor, all from a woman's perspective. Other journalists called the paper "lively and readable," concerned with "the news of an active reform movement and calling unsympathetic critics to account."

"Calling critics to account" wasn't ladylike. Anthony and Stanton's political actions began to alienate other suffragists. The argument came to a head at the 1869 American Equal Rights Association convention. Frederick Douglass asked woman suffragists to hold their demands to vote until African Americans were enfranchised. The wrongs against blacks, he explained, were great. Anthony retorted, "With all the wrongs and outrages that he today suffers, [Douglass] would not exchange his sex and take the place of Elizabeth Cady Stanton." Douglass did not deny her claim. But he didn't back down. Lucy Stone couldn't choose sides. She wanted equal rights for all, but admitted she would "be thankful in my soul if anybody can get out of the terrible pit."

Wounded by the lack of solidarity, Anthony and Stanton decided to fight fire with fire. Since the politicians wanted specialized federal amendments, Anthony and Stanton would lobby for a national woman suffrage amendment. They obviously couldn't count on AERA members, so Anthony and Stanton cofounded the National Woman Suffrage Association (NWSA). AERA members who did not believe in their move stayed with Lucy Stone.

The Revolution had 2,000 subscribers even after the split. By 1870, it had 3,000 readers. Female workers could always find news of labor unions and reports on labor conditions and educational opportunities for working women there. Then Train's financial support of the paper ended. Anthony couldn't find many reliable advertisers, and subscriber money simply wasn't enough. Printing costs put Anthony deeper and deeper into debt. Finally, in May 1870, she sold the paper for $1 because this was all anyone would pay for a paper that couldn't make money. Anthony kept the paper's $10,000 debt.

But something good seemed to come from the hated 14th and 15th amendments. The 14th Amendment gave citizenship and citizens' rights to "all persons born or naturalized in the United States," then decreed that all male citizens had the right to vote. The 15th emphasized that citizens could vote regardless of "race, color or previous condition of servitude." No mention was made of gender. One year after the 15th Amendment's 1870 approval, a woman named Victoria Woodhull somehow got an audience with the House Judiciary Committee. There, she argued that women were citizens

The preamble of the Federal Constitution says: We, the people of the United States . . . It was we, the people, not we, the white male citizens, nor we, the male citizens; but we, the whole people, who formed this Union.

—Susan B. Anthony

and therefore entitled to the vote as outlined in the 14th Amendment. Anthony postponed the morning session of her national convention to hear Woodhull's speech. That afternoon, Anthony rallied the convention to follow Woodhull's lead and seize their rights. She spurred them to vote in the next election.

Anthony and three of her sisters made national headlines for doing just that in 1872. So did women across the country. But, unlike most of those women, Anthony was arrested. Unlike any other defendant, Anthony was tried by a self-righteous judge who ignored the jury's decision. Americans were outraged.

Anthony knew that juries were told to ignore unjust laws. That's why she'd counted on a jury trial. She'd spent the year between her arrest and trial speaking about her case all over New England, hoping to educate potential jurors. When the judge ignored the jury's decision and gave Anthony a guilty verdict and a fine she refused to pay, he was lambasted by newspaper editorials. The headlines gave suffrage public awareness and sympathy it had never enjoyed before. Woodhull's inspiration had been worthwhile. Even so, Anthony cooled toward her. Woodhull wanted suffragists to work for a suffrage president—Woodhull herself. Anthony thought a national amendment had the best chance of success.

Other suffragists snubbed Woodhull because she was divorced and spoke frankly about sex and marriage. But Anthony spoke bluntly, too. In 1871, Anthony arrived in San Francisco with Stanton just as scandal broke regarding a wealthy attorney murdered by a prostitute named Laura Fair. Anthony told a crowd of 1,200 that the fault was with a society where women couldn't earn a living except by prostitution. "If all men had protected all women as they would have their own wives and daughters protected," Anthony proclaimed, "you would have no Laura Fair in your jail tonight." The auditorium erupted into jeers. Anthony waited long minutes for silence to return. And then she repeated her sentence. The booing renewed. Still Anthony stood her ground. In the second silence, she slowly spoke. "If all men," Anthony said, "had protected all women . . ." This time, the audience listened. And they cheered. Such unrelenting determination was Anthony's hallmark.

Anthony knew no other way to work. She had already begun visiting state legislatures, lobbying for state adoption of a woman suffrage amendment. In 1880, she started making appearances before the U.S. Senate Judiciary Committee for what was becoming known as "the Anthony Amendment," a national woman suffrage amendment.

By this time Anthony had devoted half of her life to women's rights. Stanton's children and Lucy Stone's daughter had grown up and joined their mothers' cause. They began working to reunite the older women, including Anthony. Reconciliation began in 1887. In 1890, Anthony's group and Stone's officially merged at a national convention, becoming the National American Woman Suffrage Association (NAWSA). Stanton was the first president. When she retired in 1892, Anthony took over. She remained at the helm for eight years, retiring at age 80.

Leading women decades younger than she wasn't always easy. "There never was a young woman . . . who did not know that if she had had the management of the work from the beginning, the cause would have been carried long ago," Anthony said. "I felt just so when I was young." Younger women worried that Anthony tended to "scold" audiences. Newspaper cartoonists had a field day when Anthony interrupted a sexist minister by shouting, "You ought to be spanked!"

NAWSA's younger members were also easily embarrassed. They proved this by denouncing Stanton's *The Woman's Bible,* published in 1895. Stanton threatened to quit the group. Although Anthony had disapproved of *The Woman's Bible* herself, she had not publically denounced it and felt she must defend it. Anthony warned those who had denounced it, "You [would do] better to organize one woman on a broad platform than 10,000 on a narrow platform of intolerance and bigotry."

Throughout her presidency, Anthony supported educational reforms for women and blacks. Besides working with Stanton on a multivolume *History of Woman Suffrage*, she collaborated with Ida Husted Harper on *The Life and Work of Susan B. Anthony: A Story of the Evoluton of the Status of Women*, published in 1898. That same year, Anthony established a press bureau to feed articles on woman suffrage to the national and local press. She spent countless hours carefully preserving the story of the cause. Yet Anthony was unprepared for endings.

The 1902 death of 86-year-old Elizabeth Cady Stanton left Anthony "too crushed to speak." She wrote to Harper: "Oh, the voice is stilled which I have loved to hear for fifty years. Always I have felt that I must have Mrs. Stanton's opinion of things before I knew where I stood myself."

Anthony is the first and only woman ever to be honored on a circulated U.S. coin. Unfortunately, many Americans hated "Susans." The one-dollar coins were confused with similarly sized quarters, and minting was stopped after only two years in 1980. (U.S. Mint)

But Anthony continued to work for women's rights, nationally and internationally. Wherever she went, younger women were now the ones organizing local suffrage groups, writing articles, putting up posters, and lobbying congressmen. And though young suffragists knew that if they'd "had the management . . . the cause would have been carried long ago," they showered Anthony with praise, applause, and respect. They celebrated her 86th birthday with a gala gathering. Looking around that auditorium, Anthony said, "With such women as these consecrating their lives, failure is impossible."

But after 86 years of nonstop travels and trials, Anthony would not live to see the success. She died at her home in Rochester on March 13, 1906. Hundreds came to her funeral. Many had to stand outside the overfilled church.

At the funeral, suffrage leader Anna Howard Shaw said, "Her work will not be finished, nor will her last word be spoken, while there remains a wrong to be righted or a fettered life to be freed in all the earth."

Chronology

FEBRUARY 15, 1820	Susan Brownell Anthony born in Adams, Massachusetts
1837	attends female Friends Seminary
1846	becomes head of the girls' department at Canajoharie Academy
1851	meets Elizabeth Cady Stanton
1852	attends her first women's rights convention
1853	begins lobbying New York legislature for women's rights
1854	organizes own woman's rights speaking tour
1856	becomes agent for the American Anti-Slavery Society

1866	cofounds the American Equal Rights Association (AERA)
1868	copublishes *The Revolution*; is delegate to National Labor Congress
1869	calls the first Woman Suffrage Convention in Washington, D.C.; cofounds National Woman Suffrage Association (NWSA)
1870	forms Workingwomen's Central Association
1872	is arrested for voting
1873	is tried, convicted, and fined $100 for voting; refuses to pay
1881	cowrites and publishes volume I of the *History of Woman Suffrage*
1890	National American Woman Suffrage Association (NAWSA) formed; Anthony elected vice president
1892	is elected NAWSA president
1898	establishes national woman suffrage press bureau; *The Life and Work of Susan B. Anthony* is published
1900	Anthony retires as president of NAWSA
MARCH 13, 1906	Susan B. Anthony dies at home in Rochester, New York

Further Reading

Barry, Kathleen. *Susan B. Anthony: A Biography of a Singular Feminist.* New York: New York University Press, 1988. A detailed adult biography that offers commentary on Anthony's society and personal psychology. Formal in style, but not overly difficult.

Gehret, Jeanne. *Susan B. Anthony: And Justice for All.* Fairport, N.Y.: Verbal Images Press, 1994. A lively, well-written biography for young readers.

Kendall, Martha E. *Susan B. Anthony: Voice for Women's Voting Rights.* Springfield, N.J.: Enslow, 1997. For younger readers.

Kraditor, Aileen, editor. *Up from the Pedestal: Selected Writings in the History of American Feminism.* New York: Fitzhenry & Whiteside, Ltd., 1968. Documents, letters, and speeches spanning four decades make up this college text. Includes brief, insightful introductions to each writing. Anthony's stump speech after her 1872 arrest for voting is edited, but still shows her scholarly approach. Also included is Anthony's 1875 support of suffrage as a cure for prostitution.

Lutz, Alma. *Susan B. Anthony: Rebel, Crusader, Humanitarian.* Boston: Beacon Press, 1959. Adult book focusing on many details of the suffrage campaign, including Anthony's dealings with other suffragists. Conversational style includes many quotes from period documents.

Stanton, Elizabeth Cady. *Eighty Years and More.* Boston: Northeastern University Press, 1993 (reprinted from 1898 original). Stanton's flowery autobiography for adults includes two loving chapters and many references to "Miss Anthony."

Sojourner Truth traveled the country speaking about the God she believed in and the world she thought God wanted, where blacks, women, and all people were treated equally. To raise money and still speak for free, she sold postcard-sized photos of herself at appearances. (Diana Star Helmer collection)

SOJOURNER TRUTH

(C. 1797–1883)

S ojourner Truth stood six feet tall, by most people's guess. She was certainly taller than most women, and taller than most men. She was stronger, too, after 30 years in slavery, working as hard as any man. Her frame was athletic, her arms were thick, even her voice was deep. Her words were also unexpected. Sojourner Truth couldn't read or write, but she knew the Bible better than folks who could. She knew the words, she knew their meaning. Most people had never heard a black woman preach, but Truth's speech was as keen as any man's.

As she spoke to a crowd one evening in Indiana, a doctor called out what others were thinking: "Your voice is not the voice of a woman." He demanded that Truth "expose her breast to the gaze of some of the ladies present so that they may report back and dispel the audience's doubts."

Truth's companions shouted their disgust. The crowd erupted in debate. As the hubbub was subsiding, Truth spoke.

She had fed "many a white babe" at her breast during slavery, Truth said. Those children were now grown, and though they'd drunk the milk of a black woman, she knew those children were better men than the doctor and his like. Her hand moved to her buttons as she spoke.

"I will show my breast to the entire congregation," she said. "It is not my shame, but yours."

Sojourner Truth was born between 1797 and 1800 in Ulster County, New York. No one knows exactly when. The day, the month, the year of a slave's birth didn't matter to the owner. The date mattered to her parents, Maumau Bett and Baumfree, but like most slaves, they didn't know how to read or write to record their baby's birth.

She was named Isabella Hardenbergh, because her family belonged to the Hardenberghs. She learned the Hardenbergh's language, Dutch, and spoke English with a Dutch accent till she died. Isabella, called Belle, was Baumfree and Maumau Bett's 10th child. Their other children were sold before Belle knew them. Another baby, Peter, was born when Belle was little. They lived in the Hardenbergh's dank cellar, crowded with other slaves. Belle remembered loving her parents, who told her stories about God, and fearing the Hardenberghs, who might sell her as they'd sold the other children.

That fear came true in 1806, when Charles Hardenbergh died. Belle's father was too old to work, so he was set free. Maumau Bett was freed, too, to support him. But they had no jobs, no money, no home. They continued living in the basement, doing odd jobs for small pay. Belle was sold at auction to a family who didn't speak Dutch.

When she didn't understand, Belle's new owners beat her till she bled. Her father did the only thing in his power to help: He found another white man to buy her. Belle visited her parents whenever she could after that. But by 1809, both were dead, of poverty and neglect.

Belle was close to six feet tall before she was 15. That made her attractive to farmers needing field hands. In 1810, John Dumont bought her. Dumont loved to brag that Belle worked as hard as any man. But her hard work didn't help when she fell in love with Robert, a slave from another farm. Slaves were allowed to marry only their own master's slaves, so Belle was told to marry a man named Thomas in 1814. Over the next 12 years, they had five children together. Belle named them for the lost members of her family.

In 1817, Belle heard miraculous news. New York State promised abolition—freedom for all its slaves—in 10 years. The promise made those years more bearable. Then, in 1825, Dumont offered Belle liberty one year sooner in exchange for extra hard work. Belle kept her promise. Dumont didn't keep his. Belle wasted no more words on him.

She fled Dumont's farm with her baby Sophia in 1826, a year before slavery was abolished in New York. She left the other children with their father. As she said years later, "Sisters, if women want any more rights than they've got, why don't they just take them and not be talking about it?"

Belle had taken what she knew was hers. Dumont came after her, but a Quaker family named Van Wagener took her in and even paid Dumont for her freedom. Gratefully, she stayed and worked for them until that wonderful day—Freedom Day—in 1827. But when Belle went to see her children at Dumont's, her son was gone. Dumont had illegally sold five-year-old Peter out of state, to someone in Alabama, where Peter would never be free. An enraged Belle grilled the Dumonts about Peter's location, but they didn't understand. To them, Peter wasn't anyone's cherished son. They described him as "a paltry little nigger."

But Belle "felt the power of a nation was with me." And she was not alone. The Van Wageners and other Quakers in Ulster County, New York, helped Belle hire a lawyer. They advised her and gave her places to sleep, but it was Belle who trekked on foot from town to town, from office to intimidating office, repeating her story and following instructions and waiting for the lengthy "process of law."

> I have heard the Bible, and have learned that Eve caused man to sin. Well, if the first woman God ever made was strong enough to turn the world upside down all alone, these women together ought to be able to turn it back and get it right side up again.
>
> —Sojourner Truth

Belle was awarded her son because it was illegal to sell him out of state. She was one of the first black women in America to win a court case against a white man.

Belle and Peter lived with the Van Wageners a while in Ulster County, close to Belle's other children. But by 1828, she knew her bright son needed more. She moved with him to New York City, where one of Truth's church friends sponsored him in school.

Truth's domestic work kept her near her son. She worked with charities, too, and in 1832 met two men forming a new church. One man claimed to be John the Baptist. The other said he was God. Belle believed in miracles. She joined their plan to build "The Kingdom of God," a community that would be heaven on earth in Sing Sing (Ossining), New York. Others invested money in the scheme. Belle could only give her labors as a cook and housekeeper, and for months she did, the only black woman in The Kingdom.

But then her doubts began. Belle left The Kingdom just before one of the leaders suddenly died and his scam was exposed. Newspapers were filled with word of the scandal, especially after two Kingdom members wrote a novel based on their experience. In their story, a religious con man is murdered by a maid—the only maid and the only black woman in the story. Like many novels of the 1800s, this one was printed in newspapers. As sometimes happens even today, people believed the novel was true.

Belle didn't have money or property. All she had was an honorable name. She gathered letters commending her character and sued the newspaper. In 1835, she won a second court case against a white man, this time for $125.

Just when Belle's life seemed better, Peter's got worse. He wouldn't go to school or work. He stole and lied. A judge finally ordered him to work on a ship. Peter sailed away, and Belle never saw him again.

Belle and her son were free, yet they were separated, as Maumau Bett had been separated from her children. Their separation made Belle realize that she was still a slave. She was enslaved by jobs and earning money, by life in New York City where she said "the rich rob the poor and the poor rob one another." She was enslaved by her own thoughts, by what she thought was possible. She broke those chains in 1843. She packed a pillowcase and "left the house of bondage," walking away from New York. She didn't tell her children where she was going, because she didn't know herself.

"I left everything behind. I wa'n't goin' to keep nothin' of Egypt on me," she told activist Lucretia Mott years later. "So I went to the Lord and asked him to give me a new name. And the Lord gave me Sojourner, because I was to travel up and down the land showin' the people their sins and bein' a sign unto them. Afterward, I told the Lord I wanted another name, 'cause everybody else had two names. And the Lord gave me Truth, because I was to declare the truth to the people." Sometimes, she said her last name was the same as her master's.

At first, Truth's gospel was spread quietly. She traveled, spent the night with a family, and moved on. Then she discovered camp meetings, popular gatherings of traveling preachers. Here, she shared her "truths," the stories of her life. Truth's stories of beatings, separations, and desperation shocked her New England listeners, yet she left them with hope. For Truth assured them, "I talks to God. And God talks to me."

Religious meetings were popular in the 1840s, and people began to know Truth's name. She developed a reputation for facing down hecklers and even hostile crowds, for many Americans couldn't see past her skin and old-fashioned Quaker dress. "I cannot read a book," she once said, "but I can read the people." She sang to crowds like a mother to her children. She told a hissing crowd, "I know it feels a kind of hissin' and ticklin' to see a colored woman get up and tell you about things . . . but we have been long enough trodden now, we will come up again, and now I am here."

When Truth didn't find a meeting, she created one herself. She always spoke for free and made money for food by selling photographs of herself. The inscription read, "I sell the shadow to support the substance." In 1850, she told her life story for publication. She sold *The Narrative of Sojourner Truth* for money to live on and to save for a house she hoped to buy near her daughters.

*W*here did your *Christ come from? From God and a woman. Man had nothing to do with him!*

—Sojourner Truth

Truth's *Narrative* embodies the problem of capturing Truth's history. Since Truth could not read or write, others had to be trusted to record her words. Accounts of the same speech, transcribed by two different people, seem to have been spoken by two different people. This is especially true of Truth's most famous speech.

She appeared, unexpectedly, at the Women's Rights Convention in Akron, Ohio, in 1851. The year before, Truth had attended her first women's rights meeting. She'd realized that women of all colors answered to husbands and fathers the way slaves answered to masters. And to Truth, that was wrong. In Akron, she found male speakers attacking women's rights, while most of the women were too proper to speak in public. Yet they didn't want Truth to defend them. Their cause was a touchy subject by itself, without linking it to the abolition of slavery. But Truth asked to speak and then rose.

The accounts of what she said hold the same thoughts and meanings but vary widely in power and beauty. The *Anti-Slavery Bugle*'s unadorned report was printed one month after Truth's speech. Another reporter, Frances Dana Gage, did not publish her version for 30 years. Gage wrote at least partly from memory, and the words she attributed to Truth had music and meaning only hinted at in the *Bugle*. Yet the *Bugle* began its story by admitting: "It is impossible to transmit [Truth's speech] to paper, or convey any adequate idea of the effect it produced upon the audience. Those only can appreciate it who saw her powerful form, her whole-souled, earnest gesture, and listened to her strong and truthful tones."

Gage's retelling conveys that strength. "Well, children," Truth began, as she often did. ("You are somebody's children," she sometimes explained.) "Where there is so much racket there must be something out of kilter. . . . But what's all this talking about? That man over there says that women need to be helped into carriages and lifted over ditches, and to have the best place everywhere. Nobody ever helps me into carriages or over mud puddles, or gives me any best place. And a'n't I a woman?"

She pushed up her sleeve. "Look at me. Look at my arm! I have plowed and planted and gathered into barns, and no man could head me! And a'n't I a woman? I could work as much and eat as much as a man, when I could get it, and bear the lash as well. And a'n't I a woman?" Then she turned to the men who said that women should devote themselves to their children. "I have borne thirteen children and seen them most all sold off into slavery. And when I cried out with my mother's grief, none but Jesus heard me. And a'n't *I* a woman?"

Truth had five children. Her mother lost thirteen. Truth enlarged her own loss to include her mother's loss to help listeners understand the vastness of a mother's grief.

"As for this thing in the head," she said, "that's right, intellect—what's that got to do with women's rights, or nigger's rights? If my cup won't hold but a pint, and yours holds a quart, wouldn't you be mean not to let me have my little half-measure full?"

To Gage, Truth's talk was the core of the meeting. Gage agreed with Harriet Beecher Stowe, the famed author of *Uncle Tom's Cabin*, who met Truth in 1853. Stowe wrote that she'd never met "anyone who had more of that silent and subtle power which we called personal presence than this woman."

By 1857, Truth thought she was ready to retire from speaking and enjoy her family. She bought a house in Battle Creek, Michigan, and her children began moving near her. But the country was restless, and Truth could sense it. In 1859, she heard Frederick Douglass tell a crowd of blacks that there was no hope for freedom without violence. "Frederick!" Truth burst out. "Is God dead?" To Truth, God was hope.

Both Truth and Douglass were right. Hope lived, but the Civil War came. And Truth sojourned again. She spoke to urge the end of slavery. She spent her money on presents for soldiers, who lined up when she came to their camps so she could speak to them, one by one. She sang spirituals, sometimes with words of her own, to give the soldiers hope. But the war did not end when the Emancipation Proclamation freed American slaves in 1863. Not knowing

> *Children, if you have woman's rights, give it to her, and you will feel better. You will have your own rights, and they won't be so much trouble.*
>
> —Sojourner Truth

where to go or what to do, blacks poured into the nation's capital. Their camp became known as Freedmen's Village. Truth went to help teach them to live free, to use foods and goods that had never been available to them before.

Most of all, Truth set an example of freedom. Washington street-cars would not stop for her, an old black woman traveling the great city. When Truth managed to jump aboard a car, she was often banished to the back or commanded to stand. One conductor shoved the old woman so hard he dislocated her shoulder. Truth filed—and won—her third court case against a white man in 1865. "The inside of the cars looked like pepper and salt,"—black and white together—she said afterward. Soon, laws were passed to undo her work, making segregation legal. But by then, Truth was fighting another battle.

Woman suffragists and abolitionists faced off in 1867 over the proposed 14th Amendment to the Constitution, which promised rights to black men but not to any women. Even Frederick Douglass, so long a friend to women, told the American Equal Rights Association convention in New York City that this was "the Negro's hour." Truth was the perfect person to rebuke him.

"I come from . . . the country of the slave," Truth told the convention. "I feel that if I have to answer for the deeds done in my body just as much as a man, I have a right to have just as much as a man. There is a great stir about colored men getting their rights, but not a word about the colored women. If colored men get their rights, and not colored women theirs, you see the colored men will be masters over the women, and it will be just as bad as it was before. So I am for keeping the thing going while things are stirring," she said. "Because if we wait till it is still, it will take a great while to get it going again."

Truth was 70 years old, but she felt "the power of a nation" still, pushing her to help. Truth saw blacks repeating her own parents' lives. They'd gone from being enslaved to whites to being enslaved by poverty. "Now some people say, 'Let the blacks take care of themselves,'" Truth said. "But you've taken everything away from them. They don't have anything left. I say, get the black people out of Washington! Get them off the government. Get the old people out

On February 4, 1986, Truth was honored with her own commemorative U.S. postage stamp. She could not read or write, but the words she spoke are still remembered. (Stamp Design © 1986 U.S. Postal Service. Reproduced with permission.)

and build them homes in the West, where they can feed themselves. Lift up those people and put them there. Teach them to read part of the time and teach them to work the other part of the time. Do that, and they will soon be a people among you."

Land in the western United States was open for settlement, and Truth asked the government to truly end slavery by giving each black family "40 acres and a mule." In 1870, she took her plan to President Ulysses S. Grant. When he failed to act, Truth, who had been a slave for 30 years, addressed the United States Congress. She dressed as plainly as she dressed for any meeting. She spoke as plainly to elected officials as she spoke to the people they represented. Congress wanted proof of support for Truth's plan. So Truth had a petition drafted and, at age 70, began one last sojourn to solicit signatures, beginning in Providence, Rhode Island. One year later, having traveled hundreds of miles and gathered thousands of signatures, she returned to the capital. But the senator who supported her plan had died, and so did Truth's idea.

She went home to Battle Creek, Michigan. Her dear grandson Sammy, who read and wrote for her, was sick. Truth cared for him until his death in 1875. She sometimes went out speaking after that, to women's rights conventions or to blacks, but not often. Truth's own health was failing. She was old. Like her mother, Truth had sores on her legs that would not heal. She died in Battle Creek on November 26, 1883.

When Sojourner Truth changed her name, she changed her way of life. She no longer followed any prophet or employer. She didn't limit herself to one cause. Truth found work to do and she did it. She wasn't embroiled in bureaucracy or organizations. She refused to honor arbitrary, unjust rules.

"I *am* a woman's rights," Sojourner Truth once said. "I am a woman's rights."

Chronology

CIRCA 1797	Isabella Hardenbergh born in Ulster County, New York
1810	is sold to John Dumont
1814	marries Thomas, a slave; they have five children together
1826	leaves Dumont farm when Dumont breaks promise to free her early; is "sold" to Isaac Van Wagener along with her baby Sophia
1827	officially freed from slavery; files suit to reclaim her son Peter and wins
1833–34	lives in New York religious commune; sues reporter and wins $125

1843	leaves New York City; takes name Sojourner Truth; begins itinerant preaching
1850	*The Narrative of Sojourner Truth*, told to Olive Gilbert, is published and sold by Truth at her lectures
1851	"A'n't I a Woman" speech in Akron, Ohio
1857	moves to Michigan; buys house
1861	Civil War begins; Truth visits soldiers
1864	meets President Abraham Lincoln; begins work with freedmen
1865	13th Amendment to the U.S. Constitution, freeing all U.S. slaves, is ratified; Truth sues streetcar conductor for assault and battery
1867	addresses American Equal Rights Association (AERA) convention
1870	meets President Ulysses S. Grant; speaks to Congress, proposing freed slaves be given western land; begins petition for this land
NOVEMBER 26, 1883	Sojourner Truth dies in Battle Creek, Michigan

Further Reading

Carney, Jessie, editor. *Epic Lives: 100 Black Women Who Made a Difference.* Detroit: Visible Ink Press, 1993. A concise view of Truth's life, with comments about the society she lived in.

Lerner, Gerda. *Black Women in White America: A Documentary History.* New York: Vintage Books, 1972. Speeches, writings, letters, and reports of American black women, both famous and unknown. Sources are cited and introduced with brief historical context.

Macht, Norman L. *Sojourner Truth: Crusader for Civil Rights.* New York: Chelsea House, 1993. A brief, well-written biography for young readers.

McKissack, Patricia C. and Frederick. *Sojourner Truth: Ain't I A Woman?* New York: Scholastic, 1992. A biography for young adult readers that provides historical background to Truth's life with ample documentation and photographs.

Truth, Sojourner, as told to Olive Gilbert. *The Narrative of Sojourner Truth.* New York: Vintage Books, 1993 (reprint). Narrated as much by Gilbert as by Truth. Gilbert's views show readers the attitudes that surrounded Truth. Originally published in 1850, so events after that are not included. Also overlooked is The Kingdom scandal.

LUCY STONE

(1818 – 1893)

Before she was 21, Lucy Stone had nursed two of her sisters when they were ill and after their deaths had cared for their children. Visiting their graves, she could not even mourn their names. Their traditional tombstones read only "Wife of . . ."

Stone decided never to marry. She wouldn't give up what was hers—her earnings, her property, her identity. Stone was in love with principles.

But then she fell in love with a man.

Stone married Henry Blackwell in 1855. She did not change her name. She just called herself "Mrs." instead of "Miss." She kept her property, though law required she sign documents "Lucy Stone, wife of Henry Blackwell." Stone even sacrificed her first chance to vote rather than sign her name "Lucy Stone Blackwell." To her, women voting meant that women mattered. It was unimportant which men they were attached to.

Stone's convictions puzzled legal clerks. No woman in the United States had ever kept her birth name after marriage. More

Lucy Stone is believed to be the first woman to give a public speech for women's rights. Her 1847 address preceded the first woman's rights convention in 1848. (Oberlin College Archives, Oberlin, Ohio)

than 100 years later, the act was still uncommon. But by then there was a name for married women who kept their names. They were called "Lucy Stoners."

☆ ☆ ☆

Lucy Stone was born on August 13, 1818, near West Brookfield, Massachusetts. Her parents, Hannah and Francis Stone, headed a typical 19th-century family. Hannah kept the household running day to day and tended to their nine children, but, as Lucy Stone later said, "There was only one will in our home, and that was my father's." Francis Stone controlled the family budget so tightly that his wife "stole" cheese she'd made herself to sell for pocket money. He was often "cross with cider [drunk]," according to Lucy, who added that she "knew his slaps." But her own brawls with other children were the stuff of family legends.

Francis Stone didn't believe in college for his daughters, though he expected them to help earn money for their brothers' education. He said the Bible intended men to lead their families. Lucy didn't believe him. She suspected the original Bible suffered from poor translation. In school, she'd learn to translate it herself.

She gathered and sold wild chestnuts to buy textbooks for her precollege courses. She earned college money by teaching. Sixteen-year-old Stone's first teaching job was in a country school that was reputed to be full of bullies. The boys towered over her as she walked into the classroom her first day. Stone called the first name on the roll. Before calling another name, Stone talked with that first student. She asked friendly questions. She listened. She did the same with each student—and found no troublemakers.

Although she saved some money from teaching, Stone did not go to college right away. Two of her sisters had died, leaving young children to care for. It wasn't until 1843 that Stone was able to enroll at Ohio's Oberlin College, a rare school that accepted female students. But any hopes Stone had for gender equality ended when a professor spoke on "Woman's Rights and Duties." He sounded like Stone's father. Stone voiced her objections in class, an act few male students would hazard, and the tempo was set for her Oberlin years.

When Stone wasn't allowed to take speech and debate classes, she formed her own women's debate club. The school's Ladies Board reprimanded her. Even students seemed skeptical at first. One of Oberlin's best male speakers challenged Stone to debate whether voting would "unsex" women. Afterward, he confessed, "She had my arguments unsexed."

Stone graduated in 1847 at age 29, becoming the first female college graduate from Massachusetts. She refused to let a professor

> *The great majority of women are more intelligent, better educated, and far more moral than multitudes of men whose right to vote no man questions.*
>
> —Lucy Stone

read her graduation essay at commencement. Male students read their own papers, and Stone would leave her thoughts unspoken before she'd let someone else speak for her. In fact, Stone had decided to become a professional speaker. She gave her first public address outside Oberlin at her brother's Massachusetts church that year. Historians believe Stone was the first woman ever to speak on women's rights in public.

Stone chose her profession well. Speakers were popular entertainment in the mid-1800s. Before radio and television, when reading material was precious and live theater was rare, speakers linked isolated towns to the world. Most Americans had never seen a woman speak in public, so Stone's mere presence guaranteed curious crowds. Two antislavery societies offered Stone speaking jobs before she graduated.

If audiences came first for the novelty, the power of Stone's words drew them back. Her voice was called beautiful, eloquent, silvery. Her "very look suggests a home and a husband and a baby," wrote one reviewer. Most winsome of all, though, was Stone's love for her work. She believed in the topics she spoke about, women's rights and abolition of slavery. Likewise, she cherished audiences; she called speaking to them "my natural way." She did not use notes or memorize speeches, but spoke simply, from her heart, often for two hours. Every speech gave Stone "more and more . . . faith in myself and brave courage . . . which made me better, and was good for others too."

The tours arranged for Stone often furnished a host instead of a hotel. She stayed with plain folks and the well-to-do. Observing their different lives made Stone think more deeply about women's rights. Her thoughts came out in her speeches. When her employer asked her to focus more on abolition, Stone left their payroll to give more attention to women's rights. Quickly, the antislavery society compromised. Stone was rehired as a weekend abolitionist. During the week, she would speak about women.

Stone attended her first national convention for woman's rights in 1850 in Worcester, Massachusetts. Prominent women shared the speakers' platform. One was Antoinette Brown, Stone's best friend from college. Stone and Brown corresponded faithfully as Stone became a speaker and Brown became America's first ordained female minister. Yet Stone hesitated when asked to speak at Brown's church in 1852. By then, Stone was completely devoted to women's rights. Sometimes, that meant questioning church teachings on women. Sometimes it meant defying social expectations of women, for example, by shunning the long skirts and hair that were fashionable but inconvenient. Stone wore the knee-length "Bloomer dress" and cut her hair short. But she worried about appearing in church that way. Brown assured her famous friend that the congregation already knew "that you wear bloomers and are an infidel."

Indeed, Stone was well known by this time. In 1853, she toured New England and the Midwest and visited Ottawa, Canada, where she addressed the parliament. Newspapers, large and small, ran accounts of her speeches. When they didn't, Stone herself sometimes distributed reports by using her lecture profits, as she did after the 1850 convention. Many people met Stone in person when she organized local groups to lobby for fair laws for women. In 1853, Stone set an example by asking the Massachusetts legislature for an amendment for women's civil rights.

Stone loved her working life. That was one reason she and Brown had once promised each other never to marry. But by 1853, Stone confessed to her friend that being single was "a wretchedly unnatural way of living." Soon after, she met Henry Blackwell.

Blackwell was an entrepreneur, a businessman always experimenting with new ways to earn money. He was also a part-time speaker on abolition and women's rights. He and Stone began corresponding, for her career kept her traveling. They became friends. But even before a courtship began or Blackwell had proposed, Stone was troubled by Blackwell's inner conflicts between money and morals. Blackwell once helped a slave escape to freedom in a public railway station. Stone was electrified by Blackwell's bravery and principles. But soon after, Blackwell fretted that his action might damage his business relations. His confession was a blow to Stone.

There were other, older reasons she refused Blackwell's proposals. Stone knew that married women had no right to property. She knew married women were expected to give up their own names and pursuits. Once married, women had no power to end the union. And Stone refused because marriage meant children. At this time, abstinence was the primary form of birth control. If Stone married, she might "go out of my body [die] or have it left a wreck" in childbirth. She'd seen both happen to women she loved. Even if Stone were lucky, children would mean surrendering her life to raising them.

Yet Stone's gender had kept her from investing or managing her earnings, anyway. She'd delegated those tasks to trusted men. And Blackwell promised her that his idea of marriage "involves no sacrifice of individuality but its perfection—no limitation of the career of one or both, but its extension . . . I would not even consent that my wife should stay at home to rock the baby when she ought to be off addressing a meeting or organizing a society." Blackwell's aspirations for wealth sometimes disappointed Stone, but he was young, not quite 30 years old, and she was 36.

By November 1854, Lucy Stone had made the difficult decision to marry. Throughout her life, she was surprised that the charming Blackwell "should have married so grim a person as myself."

> F*or woman possesses every human faculty. No man would admit, even to himself, that his mother is not capable of rational choice. And if the woman he has chosen for a wife is a fool, that fact lies at least as much against his ability to make a rational choice as against hers, and should accordingly put them both into the class of excepted persons.*
>
> —Lucy Stone

At their wedding ceremony on April 29, 1855, Stone and Black-well read their own "protest against rules and customs which are unworthy of the name, since they violate justice, the essence of law." Their marriage was to be "an equal and permanent partner-ship." Stone did not promise to "obey" her husband, and she did not give up her name to take his.

She didn't give up her work, either. Stone immediately started planning the 1855 National Women's Rights Convention, set for Cincinnati. She directed the event but did not plan to speak until another presenter's words moved her to the platform. Stone's unre-hearsed words at this convention are some of her best remembered.

"The last speaker alluded to this movement as being that of a few disappointed women," Stone told the crowd. "From the first years to which my memory stretches, I have been a disappointed woman . . . In education, in marriage, in religion, in everything, disappointment is the lot of woman. It shall be the business of my life to deepen this disappointment in every woman's heart until she bows down to it no longer."

As she so often had, Stone described women's mistreatment in employment, pay, education, and marriage. She tied them all together, saying, "Woman must marry for a home, and you men are the sufferers by this; for a woman who loathes you may marry you because you have the means to get money which she cannot have. But when woman can enter the lists [contest] with you and make money for herself, she will marry you only for deep and earnest affection. . . ."

But Stone was learning that even "deep and earnest affection" didn't ensure a trouble-free marriage. Though Blackwell had promised choosing a home would be a mutual decision, he was hungry to invest in western real estate. In January 1856, Stone moved with him to Wisconsin. The remote location halted her speaking career for one long, trying year. Mail was so slow, Stone couldn't even help plan that year's woman's rights convention until she traveled back east in August.

By January 1857, Stone was lecturing on tour again. She continued even after learning she was pregnant. But she bought a small farm in Orange, New Jersey, where she intended to raise food and her child. This was a clear signal to Blackwell that, to Stone, the East Coast was home.

Their daughter, Alice Stone Blackwell, was born on September 14, 1857. That winter, Stone's new farm was sold at auction when she refused to pay the taxes on it. Her protest was based on the Declaration of Independence: "Taxation without representation is tyranny." Newspapers eagerly spread the word, and so did Stone, who left the baby with relatives as she went on a speaking tour. But Stone was torn now. She and Blackwell were learning to pursue separate lives while exchanging frequent letters. Leaving Alice was different. After being separated from her baby, Stone wrote to Antoinette Brown: "For these years, I can only be a mother—no trivial thing, either." Stone said of her child, "This work will be worthy work to leave as my last."

Stone's decision aggravated Susan B. Anthony. Stone and Anthony had worked together for more than five years now, planning conventions by mail, lecturing together, organizing, and lobbying. They considered themselves the "two wheelhorses" pulling the "chariot" of the women's rights movement. Elizabeth Cady Stanton wrote policies that steered them from her child-filled home, but it was Stone and Anthony who worked in "the field." Stone's temporary "retirement" included an occasional lecture or convention, but Anthony felt abandoned.

Stone's domestic life included more than her own child. Family members expected Stone to nurse failing relatives and adopt their orphaned children. It was 1865 before eight-year-old Alice was attending school full-time and Stone felt free to resume suffrage work full-time.

The Civil War had come and gone during Stone's recess. But Stone found that the war had created new battles for suffragists. Now that the 13th Amendment to the U.S. Constitution had freed the slaves, a proposed 14th Amendment sought to enfranchise, give the vote, to African-American men—but not women, of any color. Stone supported black suffrage, but wrote to Anthony: "These men ought not to be allowed to vote before we do, because they will be just so much dead weight to lift." She remembered earning money at Oberlin

College by teaching freedmen. These black men, who had recently been slaves, objected to being taught by a lowly woman.

In May 1865, Stone's woman's rights convention gave birth to a new group, the American Equal Rights Association (AERA). Stone lectured in New England and organized groups to spread the word for equal rights. Don't ratify an amendment, she urged state legislators, until women are included, too. By January 1867, Stone, Stanton, and Anthony had presented a petition to the New York legislature. In March, Stone addressed the New Jersey congress. By May 1867, Stone was in Kansas, where upcoming referendums included both woman and black suffrage. The state was a perfect place to prove that equal rights for all was possible.

But politicians, especially Kansas Republicans, insisted, "This is the Negro's hour." They wanted only one major change at a time.

Stone's love of people was evident, not only in her talent for public speaking, but in her devotion to her family. She found it difficult to pursue her career when her only child was young. (Burling Library, Grinnell College)

> *We are lost if we turn away from the middle principle and argue for one class . . . Woman has an ocean of wrongs too deep for any plummet, and the Negro too has an ocean of wrongs that cannot be fathomed. . . . But I will be thankful in my soul if anybody can get out of the terrible pit.*
>
> —Lucy Stone

Stone became increasingly discouraged as group after group in Kansas aligned itself with either woman suffrage or black suffrage—but seldom both. While Stone stumped for equal rights with Blackwell, Anthony canvassed other parts of Kansas with flashy millionaire Geogre Francis Train. Train supported women's rights, but Stone worried that Train's feminism was a front for his racism.

But when the hated 14th Amendment was ratified by the states in 1868, Stanton and Anthony went on the offensive. They no longer wanted to work for anything but *woman* suffrage. In fact, they would oppose measures and groups that didn't share their focus. The American Equal Rights Association wanted equal rights for all. So Stanton and Anthony left AERA in 1869 and formed their own National Woman Suffrage Association (NWSA). Their goal was another amendment, a bill for woman suffrage.

Stone believed in a constitutional amendment for woman suffrage. But she believed there were many ways to go about achieving votes for women. Legislators represented the people, after all. And lobbying person by person, state by state, was more intimate, Stone's "natural way" as a speaker. Stone and the other remaining members of AERA decided to pursue state woman suffrage referendums, too. With this new goal, the group became the American Woman Suffrage Association (AWSA). Stone and Blackwell were both active in AWSA.

Alice Stone Blackwell was 12 now. Stone began her own newspaper, *The Woman's Journal,* in January 1870 so that she could spend more time at home, near her daughter's school. She lived above the Boston office where the paper was typeset and printed by women.

She wrote, edited, and sought subscribers and advertisers herself. Yet Stone still found time that year to serve as an elected delegate to the Massachusetts Republican nominating convention. She was the first female delegate ever in the state. While Stone was presenting an ill-fated plank for woman suffrage at the convention, Blackwell took care of the paper.

Meanwhile, Stanton and Anthony had made another unfortunate friendship, this time with writer Theodore Tilton. When Tilton's fidelity to his wife came into question, NAWSA lost members. By end of 1871, 14 of 15 state suffrage societies chose affiliation with Stone's AWSA over Anthony's NWSA. But in 1872, former AWSA president Henry Ward Beecher—a well-known preacher—was accused of having an extramarital affair. By 1873, membership in Stone's group plummeted too. Suffrage had become scandalous in the public's mind. Most wealthy women wouldn't associate with an infamous cause. Working women insisted they were "suffering for bread, not for the ballot."

Stone tried to prove to women that ballots affected income. "The flour-merchant, the house-builder, and the postman charge us no less on account of our sex," she once said, "but when we endeavor to earn money to pay all these, then, indeed, we find the difference." The tax man, too, charged women no less, and Stone protested by organizing a Massachusetts antitax convention in 1874. The following year, she used her background as a teacher to develop AWSA tracts and booklets to educate the public about voting and money.

Money was a matter of principle to Stone. What mattered most to her was principle. She proved that in 1879 when she had her first chance to vote. A new Massachusetts bill allowed women to vote on school issues. Stone went to her precinct and signed her ballot. Knowing she was married, the clerk told her to add "Blackwell" after "Lucy Stone." She refused. Her vote would be nullified, he warned. But Stone's vote was her own. Just like at her Oberlin graduation, she chose to keep her voice to herself rather than have someone else represent her.

The years passed in a busy, focused hum. From Boston, Stone lobbied the state legislature, circulated equal rights petitions, and mailed pamphlets by the thousands. She edited her paper, which reported, defended, and promoted equality for women and minorities.

But Stone's health was not good. For years, she'd had stomach troubles. If she knew it was cancer, she also knew there was no treatment. Stone welcomed Alice's 1881 graduation from Boston University. Alice's return made the one-woman *Journal* into a mother-daughter operation.

When her health allowed, Stone ventured out to speak, as she did on a tour of five midwestern states in 1886. According to Alice, who traveled with her mother, "The little change and outing does her good each year. Also, it's cheering to have big audiences rise up en masse and applaud greatly when you come in, and have women who you don't know come and embrace you with tears . . . part of the affection even overflows onto me."

Time helped heal some wounds caused by different approaches to suffrage campaigning. In February 1886, Anthony's NWSA members voted to rejoin with AWSA. Four years later, reconciliation was complete. February 1890 marked the first full meeting of the National American Woman Suffrage Association, the new, reunited group. Results followed: Two years later, Stanton, Stone, and Anthony spent part of the NAWSA convention attending a House Judiciary Committee hearing on woman suffrage.

Aging and in poor health, Stone now spent most of her time reaching out to individual women. Instead of supervising the formation of local groups, she wrote hundreds of letters telling others how to lobby and raise funds. She personally mentored an ambitious young suffragist named Carrie Chapman Catt in 1891.

Stone's final weeks were spent at home in bed. Alice, at her side, took notes for *Journal* editorials until October 18, 1893, when Stone died of stomach cancer. Her last words were whispered to her only child: "Make the world better."

Chronology

AUGUST 13, 1818   Lucy Stone born near West Brookfield, Massachusetts

1847	graduates from Oberlin; begins professional speaking career; gives first known public address by woman on women's rights
1850	speaks at her first national convention for woman's rights
1853	speaks before Massachusetts legislature on behalf of amendment for full civil rights for women
1855	marries Henry Blackwell but continues lecturing; organizes Ohio National Women's Rights Convention
1856	moves to Wisconsin; speaking career comes to a halt
1857	Stone resumes public speaking; Alice Stone Blackwell born
1858	Lucy Stone's property sold at auction because she refuses to pay taxes without representation
1861	Civil War begins; Stone's suffrage work slows for baby
1865	Stone resumes full-time suffrage work
1867	Stone, Stanton, and Anthony present petition to New York legislature; Stone addresses New Jersey legislature
1869	American Woman Suffrage Association (AWSA) forms
1870	*The Woman's Journal* debuts; Stone is delegate to state Republican nominating convention
1874	Stone organizes statewide antitax convention

1879	Stone's vote annulled when she won't sign "Blackwell" on her form
1890	first full meeting of National American Woman Suffrage Association, the union of AWSA and the National Woman Suffrage Association
OCTOBER 18, 1893	Lucy Stone dies of stomach cancer at home in Boston

Further Reading

Barry, Kathleen. *Susan B. Anthony: A Biography.* New York: New York University Press, 1988. Detailed, well-documented adult book on Anthony's life. Of moderate difficulty. Good index helps locate many episodes concerning Lucy Stone and her working relationship with Anthony.

Kerr, Andrea Moore. *Lucy Stone: Speaking Out for Equality.* New Brunswick, N.J.: Rutgers University Press, 1992. Detailed account of Stone's life for adult readers. Author presents a negative view of Henry Blackwell's character, unlike authors such as Leslie Wheeler.

Kraditor, Aileen, editor. *Up from the Pedestal: Selected Writings in the History of American Feminism.* New York: Fitzhenry & Whiteside, Ltd., 1968. Documents, letters, and speeches spanning four decades make up this college text. Includes brief, insightful introductions to each writing. Stone's marriage protest and 1855 Ohio speech are included.

McPherson, Stephanie Sammartino. *I Speak for the Women: A Story about Lucy Stone.* Minneapolis: Carolrhoda Books, 1993. For younger readers.

Wheeler, Leslie, editor. *Loving Warriors: Selected Letters of Lucy Stone and Henry B. Blackwell, 1853–1893.* New York: Dial Press, 1981. Easy adult book containing correspondence between Stone and Blackwell, with ample biographical background added by editor.

VICTORIA WOODHULL

(1838–1927)

Victoria Claflin was 14, looking more like a woman than a girl—so much so that handsome Dr. Canning Woodhull proposed to her.

They'd met one month before, when Victoria had a fever. Now Woodhull had asked Victoria to go to a picnic, and there he proposed. He was schooled, well-spoken, everything she wasn't. Yet Victoria had doubts.

Her parents, reveling in Woodhull's status, did not. They didn't even want a long engagement so she would have time to get to know him better. A good match, they gloated. Marry him now.

Two months later, Victoria left her parents' house and bad name behind. She had doubts, but also a child's hope. She'd never known a family with one house instead of many evictions, with a father respected in the community and by his children. After she had given Canning his second child, Victoria had a family portrait made. They looked like a perfect family. Even though the divorce came shortly after, Victoria carried that picture for the rest of her life.

Victoria Woodhull was both famous and infamous in America for her frank discussion of sex and sex roles. This photograph was on the cover of her pamphlet, "One Moral Standard for All." (Smithsonian Institution)

Victoria Claflin was born on September 23, 1838, in Homer, Ohio. Her parents, Buck and Roxanne Claflin, were as noisy and undisciplined as their seven children. Buck scratched out a living with get-rich-quick schemes. His favorite was medicine-show man. The whole family got into this act. Son Hebern sold bogus cancer cures, while Victoria and her younger sister, Tennessee, told fortunes. The Claflins believed that both girls were clairvoyant. Victoria reported speaking with spirits of the dead, while Tennessee seemed capable of locating lost items. Such powers seldom work on command, however, so the girls learned to substitute captivating showmanship when their clairvoyance flopped.

Victoria's visions only predicted grand and good things. She didn't foresee that the doctor she married would be an alcoholic, unable to support her. When their first child was born mentally retarded one year after their wedding, Victoria blamed Canning's "disease," as she called it. She sometimes "healed" the sick in Buck's medicine show, but she couldn't heal Canning. Instead, she supported her husband and child herself, after moving them to San Francisco, a city of opportunity. Years later, Woodhull would have words for what she was learning: "Woman's ability to earn money is a better protection against the tyranny and brutality of man than her ability to vote."

In San Francisco, Woodhull was soon a rising young stage actress. But she missed her family. Her unfaithful husband wasn't a true husband. Her son Byron wasn't like other children. She went home to her unusual midwestern folks. Woodhull would never be far from her parents and sister Tennessee ("Tennie") again. Often, she supported her parents and siblings, along with her son Byron and her healthy daughter Zula.

The Claflin family business hadn't changed in her absence. Woodhull took up her old duties as a healer. She was hired in 1865 by a Civil War hero, who had both war and marital wounds. A spirit took hold of her when she first saw him, Woodhull said. The spirit said that their destinies would be bound by marriage.

Colonel James Blood was married already and so, in fact, was Woodhull. But Blood and Woodhull were both spiritualists who believed in visions. After hearing Woodhull's prophesy, Blood left his wife. Woodhull left Byron and Zula with the Claflins and ran away with him. She and Blood traveled together, she telling fortunes, he gathering crowds and money. Blood learned that the unschooled Woodhull had a spongelike memory and natural logic. Woodhull learned that Blood's respectable past as a soldier, spiritual leader, and city auditor left him hungry for meaning. He wanted to work "for the human race and not for Colonel Blood," he said. He was drawn to the way Woodhull grasped his ideals, intuitively and intelligently.

Blood divorced his wife. Woodhull divorced Canning. They filed an "intent" to marry in 1866. No records indicate they actually wed, but they believed in ties of the heart, not the law. They lived as husband and wife. Blood abandoned the proper life he'd led to became part of the Claflin medicine show.

The clamorous Claflins, with Blood and Woodhull in tow, hit broad-minded New York City in 1868. Somehow, they met 76-year-old Cornelius Vanderbilt, the richest man in America.

Historians agree that Vanderbilt was a sharp old gent. He knew that the "clairvoyant sisters," Woodhull and Claflin, were probably just gifted entertainers. But they were beautiful and appealing, and that was reason enough reason for Vanderbilt to pay them handsomely. "Tennie C." Claflin gave Vanderbilt massages to ease the pains of age. Woodhull offered him the "spirits'" insights to the future. Soon, Vanderbilt began trading predictions with Woodhull, telling her about the future of certain stocks on the market. Colonel Blood would buy or sell accordingly, using the sisters' wages from Vanderbilt. Soon, the entire Claflin clan was living the high life.

Woodhull moved into an opulent home that became a "salon," a meeting place for thinkers and activists, like Stephen Pearl Andrews. Andrews had studied world philosophies for most of his 61 years. He'd used that knowledge to create his own idealistic social system that included sexual freedom and women's rights. Woodhull, fresh from attending the 1869 National Woman's Rights Convention in New York, eagerly absorbed Andrews's thoughts. Just because Andrews had failed to make his dream of a perfect society real didn't mean it couldn't be done. Woodhull knew that reality costs money—and she just happened to have it.

By January 1870, Vanderbilt had helped Woodhull and Tennie use their stock earnings to start their own brokerage firm. The sisters had an instant customer base because Wall Street investors knew Vanderbilt was behind the scenes. "The Bewitching Brokers" made headlines across the country, and Woodhull became rich and famous.

But Woodhull knew it took more than money to make the world better. It took influence, and influence came from teamwork. Woodhull recruited another of Blood's acquaintances, Massachusetts Congressman Benjamin Butler, one of the most prominent men in Washington, where ideas and ideals were made real. Woodhull set her sights on Washington.

On April 2, 1870, a letter Woodhull wrote to the editor of the *New York Herald* was printed under the headline, "First Pronunciamento." It read:

> *All this talk of women's rights is moonshine. Women have every right. They have only to exercise them.*
>
> —Victoria Woodhull

> While others of my sex devoted themselves to a crusade against the laws that shackle the women of the country, I asserted my individual independence; while others prayed for the good time coming, I worked for it; while others argued the equality of woman with man, I proved it by successfully engaging in business; while others sought to show that there was no valid reason why women should be treated, socially and politically, as being inferior to man, I boldly entered the arena of politics and business and exercised the rights I already possessed.

Then Woodhull wrote, "I now announce myself candidate for the Presidency."

Victoria Woodhull had already done the impossible by running a successful brokerage. People couldn't dismiss the possibility she proposed now, even if they had doubts.

To support her campaign, Woodhull began publishing *The Woodhull and Claflin Weekly*. The 16-page journal focused on Woodhull's views but also included a wide range of commentary and investigative reporting. "Sixteenth Amendment" was a regular feature advocating woman suffrage. Sophisticated articles, usually written by Andrews, were printed beside stories on quacks and the occult. This odd mix gave the *Weekly* an instant, ardent readership. But Woodhull's most spectacular bid for publicity was yet to come.

Benjamin Butler was a friend of woman suffrage. He was also friend and advisor to President Ulysses S. Grant. He knew the anti-suffrage sentiments of Capitol Hill. Yet Butler wondered if the dynamic, beautiful Woodhull might actually be able to change things. Butler helped Woodhull prepare a "Memorial" to present to Congress. Her astonishing premise was that the 14th Amendment, which promised votes to all "citizens," had accidentally given women the vote.

On January 11, 1871, Woodhull was the first woman ever to address the Judiciary Committee of the House of Representatives. "I submit that I have established first, that by the mere fact of being citizens, women are possessed of the elective franchise; and second, that the elective franchise is one of the privileges of the 14th Amendment which the states shall not abridge," she said.

Susan B. Anthony and other leaders of the National Woman Suffrage Association delayed their own convention in order to see Woodhull's presentation. Afterward, Anthony burst out, "Bravo, my dear Woodhull . . . glorious old Ben [Butler]!" She swept Woodhull away to repeat the Memorial at the suffrage convention.

The congressional report on Woodhull's Memorial was short, and its reasons for rejecting her petition weak. Disenfranchising women, the majority said, was a law that states "may justly proscribe for the general good of the whole." The opinion pointed out that states excluded other citizens from voting, such as minors and lunatics. The minority opinion was lengthy and thorough. Signed by Butler and William Loughridge of Iowa, the minority backed Woodhull's words with documented legal precedents.

Women didn't become enfranchised, but "the Woodhull" became a lecture phenomenon. Suffragists' hopes soared because women had finally been heard. But some women feared Woodhull's reputation would reflect badly on them. It was common knowledge that she'd divorced Canning Woodhull and married Colonel Blood. When the penniless, ailing Canning moved back in with the Claflins, Victoria Woodhull was accused of having two husbands.

Elizabeth Cady Stanton retorted that Woodhull's love affairs would only matter "when the men who make laws for us in Washington can stand forth and declare themselves pure and unspotted from all sin. . . . We have had enough women sacrificed to this sentimental, hypocritical prating about purity," she fumed. "This is one of man's most effective engines for our division and subjugation. He creates the public sentiment, builds the gallows, and then makes us hangmen for our sex. . . . If Victoria Woodhull must be crucified, let men drive the spikes and plait the crown of thorns."

Woodhull came right out and said it: "Yes, I am a free lover." She meant she believed marriages sometimes should end, rather than continue and spread unhappiness. "I am conducting a campaign against marriage, with the view of revolutionizing the present theory and practice," she proclaimed.

She talked plainly about the kinds of freedom women sought. "Those who are called prostitutes . . . are free women, sexually, when compared to the slavery of the poor wife. They are at liberty, at least to refuse; but she knows no such escape . . . Yet marriage is held to be synonymous with morality! I say, eternal damnation sink such morality!"

Stanton, who had long lobbied for marriage reform, supported Woodhull's appearance at the 1871 National Woman Suffrage Association convention in New York City. There, Woodhull presented

Harper's Weekly, *on November 25, 1871, recreated the scene of Woodhull attempting to vote in that year's election.*   (Burling Library, Grinnell College)

a presidential platform that would seem up-to-date more than a century later. Woodhull called for police, prison, tax, welfare, and education reforms; term limits, governmental accountability, nation-wide public transportation systems, foreign trade restrictions, international relations, an eight-hour workday, minority representation, "small government," and universal suffrage. And Woodhull backed action.

"If the very next Congress refuses women all the legitimate results of citizenship," she cried, "we mean treason! We mean secession. . . . We are plotting revolution! We will overthrow this bogus Republic and plant a government of righteousness in its stead!"

Woodhull had become a riveting speaker. Insiders sometimes recognized Andrews's thoughts, or Blood's words. But biographer Emanie Sachs pointed out, "None who heard Victoria Woodhull doubted her sincerity . . . if some of the light was Stephen Pearl Andrews's, all of the heat was hers."

Staid and faint-hearted NAWSA members dropped out after Woodhull's "Great Secession" speech. Anthony became worried about Woodhull's control over the organization. She had seen suffragists lose momentum during the Civil War. Now Woodhull wanted to take energy from the cause to form a new political party to advocate her campaign. At the 1872 NAWSA convention, Anthony refused to even take a vote on the idea. The last convention was already being called "the Woodhull Convention." Anthony wanted this to be a suffrage convention.

Woodhull walked out. Many followed her, though some, like Stanton, were torn. The next day, Woodhull called her own meeting at another hall. Six hundred came, many abandoning Anthony to do so. They chose a new way to protest. They chose to use the political system to seize their rights. The new Equal Rights Party assembled, created its platform, then gave its official nomination to Victoria Woodhull. "Victoria! Victoria! Victoria!" The chant continued over cheers, handshaking, hugging, kissing, and crying. Reporters had never seen such an emotional deluge.

Woodhull's old Wall Street acquaintances were uneasy with her new role. Her presidential platform didn't always favor business, and her "revolution" might overthrow the economy that drove Wall Street. "The Lady Broker's" business began to fall off.

Woodhull was soon evicted from her home, but not because of her declining income. Her problem was a lady named Catharine Beecher.

Catharine Beecher and her sister, Harriet Beecher Stowe, were offended by Woodhull's words, her behavior, her business, and her personal life. They didn't like it that Woodhull and their brother, Henry Ward Beecher, had mutual friends. So the Beecher sisters began pressuring local landlords to refuse Woodhull refuge. They whispered that Woodhull's two husbands proved her promiscuity.

*F*riends of the cause should act in concert. Their real power has never been felt.

—Victoria Woodhull

The Beechers were prominent people. Henry Ward Beecher was a preacher of celebrity status. He was featured in the newspapers of the day, the way preachers 100 years later starred in television shows. Beecher's name was known nationwide, but in New England, where his wealthy parishioners lived, the Beecher name got results. His sisters asked landlords and hotel managers to shun Victoria Woodhull.

Evicted again and again, Woodhull finally took to sleeping with her children in the office of the *Weekly*, the one place she managed to keep. She'd had to suspend publication for a few weeks. The brokerage had folded, too. Her campaign had lost its followers. By September 1872, Woodhull had nothing left to lose. She gambled everything she had.

What she had was the truth. Henry Ward Beecher had been untrue to his wife, and most of New York society knew it. But Woodhull, who was condemned for living up to her words, blew the whistle on Beecher's hypocrisy. Beecher's treatment of his wife was exactly why Woodhull espoused free love.

Woodhull gave speeches about Beecher's illicit affairs. With her speaking fees, she revived the *Weekly* and printed the story there and was thrown in jail for "sending obscene material through the mail."

The publicity was stupendous. Single copies of the tell-all paper were "rented" for $1—more than a day's wages—and sold for $40.

The next few months were a merry-go-round of trials and jailings. The charges against Woodhull were dismissed, and her speaking schedule soared, but the stress had its effects. In June 1873, Woodhull collapsed. She went in and out of consciousness for a week. Doctors believed a blood vessel in her lungs had ruptured. Worried about losing more money to illness, Woodhull returned to the lecture podium as soon as possible that summer. Woodhull loved speaking, and audiences loved her.

A pamphlet began appearing at her talks in 1874. Published by spiritualist Dr. Joseph Treat, a one-time admirer, it accused Woodhull of prostitution. Though the Beecher case was still in court, Treat's pamphlets hurt Woodhull more. They made people doubt her dedication to free, true love. While trying to clarify her beliefs, Woodhull began sounding more conventional, conservative, even religious. Her confused following began to dissolve as her writing and lectures lost their edge. Support dwindled, killing the *Weekly* in 1876. Woodhull's marriage to Blood ended, too.

Then, Cornelius Vanderbilt died. There was talk of calling Woodhull as a witness in the heirs' debate over the sanity of his will. Woodhull never testified because, in 1877, she moved to England with her parents, her children, and Tennie. Historians have long guessed that the Vanderbilts paid her passage in return for her silence.

Woodhull soon began speaking in England. Although her 1878 speeches in Britain weren't headline grabbers, she did raise eyebrows by urging parents to teach their children about sexuality. She met John Biddulph Martin, known as "England's most eligible bachelor," after he attended one of her talks. In 1883, they married.

In 1892, Woodhull began a new publishing venture, *The Humanitarian*. Like the *Weekly*, this paper focused on an ideal society. But *The Humanitarian* was more practical during its nine years, promoting farming for women, better education for young children, and community spirit. Sometimes, an editorial hinted at Woodhull's former fire, as when she wrote in 1896: "Suffrage is only one phase of the larger question of woman's emancipation. More important is the question of her social and economic position." But for the most part, Woodhull lived quietly for the rest of her life. Her original, radical followers felt betrayed by her quietness, even by her half-hearted attempt to revive her presidential candidacy in 1892. After John Biddulph Martin's death in 1897, Woodhull spent her final days applying some of *The Humanitarian*'s theories by renting farmland to women, starting a kindergarten, and turning her barn into a village lecture hall. With daughter Zula nearby, Victoria Woodhull Martin died on June 10, 1927.

History hasn't known what to make of the woman cartoonist Thomas Nast called "Mrs. Satan." Even the inseparable Stanton and Anthony parted when it came to Woodhull. To Stanton, Woodhull was "a grand, brave woman" who "has done a work for women that none of us could have done. . . . She has risked and realized the sort of ignominy that would have paralyzed any of us . . . with a steadfast faith that glorious principle would triumph at last."

Anthony thought Stanton's "consulting and conceding to Woodhull" hurt woman suffrage. "Our movement as such is so demoralized by letting go the helm of ship to Woodhull—though we rescued it—it was as by a hair breadth escape."

Later historians have argued about Woodhull, too. Some, like Stanton, believe Woodhull revitalized a dying movement after the setback of the Civil War. Others, like Anthony, believe Woodhull's wildness gave women more obstacles to overcome. Woodhull herself changed during her life, becoming more restrained and conventional. In her early years, she argued passionately for free love. In her later years, when she wanted to live quietly, she'd answer accusations of "free love" by saying, "I never knew love was anything but free."

Critics called her immodest and unwomanly. Yet audiences could see that in many ways Woodhull personified traditional femininity. She was idealistic, emotional, and vulnerable, all the things praised in women as virtues yet used as reasons to keep them from politics. Suffragist Martha Wright called Woodhull a "true woman."

Woodhull concluded her speech "Tried as by Fire" of 1874 by saying, "So after all, I am a very promiscuous free lover. I want the love of you all, promiscuously. It makes no difference who or what you are, old or

Cartoonist Thomas Nast, famed for his version of Santa Claus, portrayed Woodhull in 1872 as an immoral demon. Unknown to most readers, Woodhull had also walked in the shoes of the woman carrying the children and drunken husband. The caption read "'Get thee behind me, (Mrs.) Satan." Wife (with heavy burden), 'I'd rather travel the hardest path of matrimony than follow your footsteps.'" (Burling Library, Grinnell College)

young, black or white, pagan, Jew, or Christian. I want to love you all and be loved by you all; and I mean to have your love."

Chronology

SEPTEMBER 23, 1838	Victoria Woodhull born in Homer, Ohio
1853	marries Canning Woodhull
1865	divorces Canning Woodhull
1866	files "intent" to marry Colonel James Blood
1870	Woodhull, Claflin & Co. opens on Wall Street; *The Woodhull & Claflin Weekly* begins publication; announces candidacy for president
1871	presents "Memorial" on woman suffrage to the Judiciary Committee of the House of Representatives
1872	forms Equal Rights Party
1873	jailed for printing and mailing account of Beecher affair
1876	divorces Blood; ceases publication of *Woodhull & Claflin Weekly*
1877	moves to England with sister Tennie
1883	marries John Biddulph Martin
1892	begins publishing *The Humanitarian*; revives presidential candidacy
1901	ceases publishing *The Humanitarian*
JUNE 10, 1927	Victoria Woodhull Martin dies

Further Reading

Arling [Emanie Sachs]. *The Terrible Siren: Victoria Woodhull.* New York: Harper & Brothers, 1928. Printed just one year after Woodhull's death, this book contains interviews with people who knew her and excerpts from publications from her lifetime. Not footnoted, but with a detailed bibliography. The old-fashioned, easy adult style of writing and illustrations gives the flavor of Woodhull's era.

Johnson, Gerald. "Dynamic Victoria Woodhull," *American Heritage,* vol. 7, no. 4, June 1956. Overview of Woodhull's life focuses on her early political career and provides contemporary social context. Moderate difficulty.

Johnston, Johanna. *Mrs. Satan: The Incredible Saga of Victoria C. Woodhull,* New York: G.P. Putnam's Sons, 1967. Adult book focusing on free love and the details of Woodhull's personal life. Speculation mixed with information; skeptical of psychic phenomenon.

Meade, Marion. *Free Woman: The Life and Times of Victoria Woodhull.* New York: Alfred A. Knopf, 1976. Young adult book includes fictionalized dialogue and dramatization.

Stern, Madeleine B., editor. *The Victoria Woodhull Reader.* Weston, Mass.: M & S Press, 1974. Woodhull's newspaper articles and speeches are reproduced here, often in the form of direct copies of the pages issued 100 years before. Brief introductions to sections by the editor provide context. Relevant contemporary rebuttals to Woodhull included. Formal Victorian language sometimes difficult.

Underhill, Lois Beachy. *The Woman Who Ran for President: The Many Lives of Victoria Woodhull.* Bridgehampton, N.Y.: Bridge Works Publishing Co., 1995. Chapters in this moderately difficult adult book cite sources with a page-coded index, not footnotes. Many period quotes. Highly detailed account focuses most on Woodhull's political life.

AMELIA JENKS BLOOMER

(1818–1894)

Petite Amelia Bloomer looked even smaller on stage in a packed auditorium. Despite her odd dress—a knee-length skirt with loose trousers underneath—she looked feminine, even attractive, nothing like the cigar-smoking "Bloomer girls" in newspaper cartoons. Audiences didn't expect a woman bold enough to speak in public to seem so ordinary.

Bloomer often greeted her listeners with "My friends!" She quoted the Bible, even St. Paul's advice to women to stay home and learn from their husbands.

Then Bloomer smiled. "If women obeyed," she said, "ministers would have but few listeners."

True, she said over the laughter that followed, the Bible taught that Adam was created before Eve. Many Christians said this proved man's dominance over woman. "Adam first, then Eve, they say," cried Bloomer. "To this we reply: Animals first—then Adam."

Bloomer's humorous logic wooed her audience. She talked of things they were familiar with, of husbands and wives, how wives took care of the homes only their husbands legally owned. Then

One of Amelia Jenks Bloomer's greatest contributions to the suffrage cause was The Lily, *a newspaper she edited and published with an all-female staff.* (Burling Library, Grinnell College)

Bloomer talked of wives left destitute when their husbands died or became alcoholics. She told of women with children to feed, unemployable because of their sex, finally desperate enough to endure the endless hours and worthless wages of a seamstress.

Bloomer's speaking skills might have been expected in a college-educated man. What she did next was not. Suddenly, unaccompanied, she sang:

Stitch! Stitch! Stitch!
in poverty, hunger and dirt—
sewing at once with a double thread
a shroud as well as a shirt.

Amelia Jenks was born on May 27, 1818, in Homer, New York, the youngest of six children. Raised by a barely successful cloth maker and his strict Puritan wife, Jenks could only attend school sporadically. The whole family helped with the home business. Even so, at age 19, Jenks was hired as a live-in governess not far from Homer. She found she didn't like most social gatherings there. Many of the people drank alcohol, and Jenks had little interest in such folks. But one, a lanky Quaker lawyer named Dexter Bloomer, kept writing her letters, convincing her that he believed in the temperate use of alcohol. Jenks married Bloomer on April 15, 1840. But Dexter Bloomer believed that "the happiest day of her life" was one year later, when he gave up alcohol for good.

The newlyweds set up housekeeping in quiet Seneca Falls, New York. Dexter had recently purchased the *Seneca County Courier* newspaper. The paper was an opportunity to promote the social reforms that the Bloomers both cared about. Amelia was often inspired with new ways to support Dexter's arguments after reading one of his articles. Her opinions were common sense and well reasoned. Dexter urged his wife to share her thoughts in his newspaper and in temperance papers such as *The Water Bucket.*

But Amelia Bloomer described herself at this time as "a shrinking, bashful woman." Because she believed putting her name in print would be unladylike, her earliest writings did not bear her name. Bloomer preferred to work quietly for her husband, the temperance cause, and the Episcopal Church. Then, in July 1848, Dexter asked her to report on a local woman's rights convention, organized by newcomer Elizabeth Cady Stanton. Bloomer said nothing at the convention. She did not even introduce herself to Stanton. But soon after, Bloomer took a giant step away from her role as a "shrinking, bashful woman."

That September, when Bloomer helped form the Ladies Total Abstinence Benevolent Society, she agreed it should have no ties to any male temperance group. Theirs was the only local society that guaranteed women the right to vote, speak, and participate in actual reform work—even in their own temperance newspaper, *The Lily*. A male lecturer passing through Seneca Falls offered to recruit subscribers from around the country. When few subscribed, Bloomer's cohorts lost interest.

But Bloomer found that she "could not so lightly throw off responsibility. Our word had gone to the public and . . . people would say it was 'just like women: what more could you expect of them?'"

She knew from her husband's work what was expected from newspaper editors: writing, reading proofs, making printing contracts, advertising for subscribers, packaging, mailing, and more. The increased load of keeping *The Lily* afloat might not have been so bad if Bloomer hadn't just started another new job—she became deputy postmistress of Seneca Falls when Dexter left the *Courier* to become postmaster. Amelia Bloomer ran the post office day to day. She wrote for her paper, at night. Elizabeth Cady Stanton couldn't catch Bloomer to introduce herself until six months after *The Lily* first appeared on January 1, 1849.

Stanton finally went the post office to offer to write for *The Lily*. Bloomer hesitated. To her, *The Lily* was a "temperance only" paper, and "was never the organ of any society, party or . . . individual but myself." Remembering Stanton's convention, Bloomer felt sure Stanton would want to write about topics besides temperance. She finally agreed to let Stanton write for *The Lily* under the name of "Sunflower." But she promised her readers that the Sunflower would vanish if it became "too proud."

Sunflower stayed, and its shadow changed *The Lily*'s growth. Before 1849 was over, Bloomer published an article on healthful clothing for women in her "temperance only" paper. By 1850, Bloomer wrote her own first non-temperance editorial, lambasting a Tennessee legislature resolution saying women had no souls.

Bloomer began exploring many ideas in the pages of *The Lily*: the benefits of women's exercise, the value of female education, the hypocrisy of punishing "fallen" women but not the men who fell with them. She didn't write or act like a "shrinking, bashful woman," but like a newspaperwoman. Newspapers were the 1800s' primary mass communication. Writers responded to competing papers' work in their own publications. In-print arguments went on issue after issue. Bloomer didn't shrink from these debates. Sometimes, she sought them out.

Bloomer spotted some February 1851 remarks from the new editor of the *Seneca County Courier*. He was writing about a fashion called the "Turkish dress." Cut near the knee, Turkish skirts had no heavy petticoats like other dresses of the time. Ladies' legs were still covered, but by wide-legged trousers. The dress's waist was loose, without fashionable waist-crunching corsets. When the *Courier* sarcastically approved of the costume, Bloomer responded in *The Lily*. "As the editor of the *Courier* was opposed to us on the women's rights question, this article of his gave me an opportunity to score him one of having gone so far ahead of us as to advocate us wearing the pantaloons. . . ."

> *Alas! poor Adam! While it required all the persuasive powers and eloquence of the subtle tempter, all the promises of wisdom and knowledge and power to seduce the so-called "weaker" vessel from the right path, all that was necessary to secure his downfall was simply to offer him the apple.*
>
> —Amelia Jenks Bloomer

The *Courier* launched a literary counterattack. Bloomer parried, and her captivated readers clamored for pictures and dress patterns.

"My subscription list ran up amazingly into the thousands" from a few hundred, Bloomer wrote. But when Elizabeth Cady Stanton appeared that spring wearing the outfit in Seneca Falls, Bloomer realized, "I had gotten myself into a position from which I could not recede if I had desired to do so." She felt she, too, should do more than just talk about reform. Before summer, Bloomer announced in *The Lily* that she, too, was wearing the Turkish dress.

She invited *Lily* readers' responses to the "reform dress" and printed many of them. A Boston physician endorsed the clothes, describing how the common fashions, weighing up to 15 pounds "supported by the hips alone . . . must embarrass the organs within the exercise of their functions." In other words, fashionable ladies were risking their health. Armed with science, Bloomer ignored the newspaper cartoons, theatrical farces, and jokes portraying pants-wearing, bullwhip-wielding women. She "continued to wear the new style on all occasions . . . For some six or eight years, or so long as I remained in active life, and until the papers ceased writing squibs at my expense, I wore no other costume," she said.

Dexter Bloomer observed that, "for better or worse," the Turkish costume was particularly attractive on the 5-foot-4-inch, 100-pound red-haired Amelia. More people began stopping by the post office in 1851; he believed it was to look at the dress. Newspaper columnists who saw Bloomer in the outfit generally agreed with her husband—while criticizing the short, stout Stanton for wearing it.

Bloomer had made the dress famous through *The Lily*, first in writing, then with her own pictured figure. So the fashion began to be called "the Bloomer dress," "Bloomer's dress," and, later, simply "bloomers." Bloomers inspired songs, dances, and even clubs. In Lowell, Massachusetts, factory girls formed "The Bloomer Institute," where bloomers symbolized women's commitment to self-improvement and independence. Small wonder: Bloomers had become a uniform for suffrage leaders Stanton, Susan B. Anthony, and Lucy Stone. Bloomer found herself among their ranks in Rochester, New York, at the 1852 spring Woman's State Temperance Society Convention. There, after "much persuasion," Bloomer gave her first public address before a crowd of 1,800.

Bloomer knew women speaking in public still seemed outrageous. But, according to her husband, "She believed most sincerely that the temperance principle of which she was an ardent advocate could never fully triumph until Woman's voice could be fully and decisively heard in its settlement." So Bloomer raised her voice. "Such thoughts as these may be thought unladylike, but if they are so, they are not unwomanly," she said. "Every woman who is tied to a confirmed

Harper's Monthly *of 1851 liked the idea of functional clothing for women but didn't quite understand that the outfit was more than short skirts. Loose-fitting waists were another important part of "bloomers," nicknamed after Bloomer's newspaper praised the outfit.* (Burling Library, Grinnell College)

drunkard should sunder the ties, and if she do it not otherwise, the law should compel it, especially if she has children."

By 1852, Bloomer proclaimed *The Lily* was "Devoted to the Interests of Woman." By 1853, she was urging *Lily* readers to "earn the right to vote" by proving their capabilities in all kinds of jobs. Bloomer practiced what she preached. With other woman's rights leaders, she held three meetings in New York City's Metropolitan Hall. They were the first women ever to address an audience of New Yorkers from a public platform. Crowds of 3,000 to 5,000 jammed the hall. Those who didn't attend could read a detailed account of "Mrs. Bloomer's Speech" in the *New York Herald Tribune*. The writer cited bursts of applause for Bloomer, three ovations in four consecutive sentences.

Despite Bloomer's expanding views on women's rights, Stanton sometimes became impatient with Bloomer's view of suffrage as a means to temperance. But at the end of 1853, the distance between Bloomer and Stanton became more than philosophical. Dexter Bloomer agreed to become the editor of a weekly temperance paper in Mount Vernon, Ohio. Amelia did not question her duty to go where her husband went, and the Bloomers left Seneca Falls.

Amelia became Dexter's assistant editor and a columnist for *The Western Home Visitor*, while continuing production of *The Lily* in Mount Vernon. It seemed practical for the two publications to share printing equipment, so Bloomer decided to prove her theory of women's capabilities. She hired a woman to set type for *The Lily*. Dexter's male typesetters went on strike.

Word spread quickly among the 6,000 residents of Mount Vernon. Public sentiment ran so high that Amelia Bloomer wrote to suffrage speaker Lucy Stone, who was lecturing nearby. Stone made a detour to Mount Vernon to speak on "Woman and Her Employment." The Bloomers credited her presence with calming public opinion enough to allow them to hire women to replace the striking workers. The offices of *The Lily* and *The Western Home Visitor* were joined. Later, men were hired, too, and Amelia Bloomer looked with pride on a room of men and women working together, "peaceable and harmoniously."

But before the year was out, the Bloomers were on the move again. Land was inexpensive in Council Bluffs, Iowa, and Dexter Bloomer was able to buy some. This move would be even harder on Amelia Bloomer: Council Bluffs was 300 miles from the nearest railroad stop. It would be impossible for her to distribute *The Lily*. If she didn't sell, *The Lily* would die.

Bloomer sold *The Lily* to Mary Birdsall of Richmond, Indiana, but continued writing for the paper for more than a year. During much of this time, the Bloomers were on the road—moving was slow in the days of horse-drawn coaches. Bloomer often arranged, or appeared at, suffrage meetings on the road. "I had never yet refused to proclaim the new doctrine of women's rights when I found people anxious to hear and opportunity offered," she wrote.

The Bloomers arrived in Council Bluffs, Iowa, in April 1855. Council Bluffs was an oasis for westward-bound pioneers, full of bootleg saloons, gambling houses, and brothels. Reformers like the Bloomers were uncommon among the town's 2,000 regular residents. That autumn, Amelia Bloomer lamented, "I judge that the Spirit of Reform does not dwell here: if so, I have not found it out. . . ."

In the coming years, however, Dexter Bloomer would practice law, sell insurance, serve as receiver of public lands, be both member and president of the Board of Education, and govern as mayor in 1869 and 1871.

Amelia Bloomer became the first Iowa resident to speak on women's rights, presenting a speech on suffrage in the Council Bluffs Methodist Church on December 7, 1855. Bloomer had long argued that suffrage was a means to temperance. But Iowa law officially prohibited alcohol. It was not a law many officials enforced, especially as far west as Council Bluffs. Even so, speaking in Iowa that night, Bloomer spoke solely of women's rights. This was a significant departure from her earlier personal philosophy.

"It will not do to say that it is out of woman's sphere to assist in making laws," Bloomer told her first Iowa audience, "for if that were so, then it should be also out of her sphere to submit to them."

One of Bloomer's listeners asked her to repeat her speech to the Nebraska legislature on January 8, 1856. Bloomer later reported, "I

*I*f then home be,
indeed, the sphere of
Woman, why has Man
so wholly failed to make
her supreme within
its limits?

—Amelia Jenks Bloomer

could see, as I proceeded with my arguments, that they were telling upon my listeners . . . but I was hardly prepared for the glorious result which followed—a result which almost proved a triumph. Near the close of the session—a session of only 40 days—a Bill giving women a right to vote came up by a special order of the House." No state or territory in the United States had woman suffrage in 1856. Though that Nebraska bill eventually failed, Bloomer and other suffragists were thrilled that the government seriously considered their cause.

Bloomer had found Midwest traveling conditions rugged. To speak in Nebraska, she'd braved temperatures of 30 below zero and had nearly capsized crossing the stormy Missouri River home. The windy plains even forced Bloomer to at last put aside the comfortable clothes that bore her name. The short bloomer skirt kept flapping up over her head. She returned to women's customary long skirts. Bloomer began speaking less and writing more. She became a correspondent for *The Mayflower*, a new women's rights paper, in 1861. She wrote letters to the editor of Council Bluff's two newspapers, as well as other Iowa periodicals. These editors often printed a response, prompting another essay from Bloomer who, according to her husband, never let comments on her work go unanswered.

Bloomer suspended suffrage work to help with Civil War relief efforts. When the war ended in 1865, Bloomer resumed her devotion to women's rights. Like other suffragists, she lambasted the proposed 15th Amendment to the Constitution for including suffrage for blacks, but not for women. The February 1867 editions of both Council Bluffs newspapers were filled with Bloomer's letters of protest: "Why was the Negro made a voter? Because, until he became such, there was no guarantee that his emancipation from slavery would not prove a cheat and a fraud." Women, too, needed proof that America's "inalienable rights" were for real, Bloomer wrote.

Although she couldn't travel to the women's rights convention in New York in 1866, Bloomer was named "vice president for Iowa" of the American Equal Rights Association (AERA), a lifetime position. (She continued the post after the group reorganized as the National Woman Suffrage Association.) After attending the 1869 New York convention, Bloomer returned to Council Bluffs to found a local suffrage society, becoming its first president in 1870. The Iowa Woman's State Suffrage Society formed that year, too. Vice president Bloomer and others spoke to a crowd of 2,000 suffragists at the state capital that June.

The state suffrage society had its first convention in Des Moines on October 19, 1871. Bloomer became the group's new president that day. The young organization spent some time voting to define its purpose and goals. "Free love," or sexual promiscuity, had recently been linked with women's rights in national headlines. Victoria Woodhull, who'd argued for woman suffrage before the U.S. House judiciary committee, was accused of having two husbands. Iowa women emphasized their thoughts on free love with a resolution stating "[we believe] that the ballot is a power to be used only in the interest of virtue and morality." One vociferous attendee demanded a harsher, even more specific resolution. But Bloomer, mindful of the evening's full convention schedule, asked that the scheduled speakers be allowed to continue. The majority of the delegates agreed, and the convention went on, with praise from the next day's *Des Moines Register* for its "decorum" and "intelligent accord."

Two days later, however, a letter to the editor of the *Des Moines Register* accused Bloomer of supporting free love, saying she'd refused to denounce Woodhull at the convention. More letters to the editor began filling papers statewide. Misunderstandings built upon hearsay. Small-town suffragists, fearing the free love label, broke from Bloomer's state group. When the Iowa Suffrage Bill was defeated on March 29, 1872, many of its supporters blamed Bloomer.

"From the enemies of the cause we may expect such things," Bloomer said, "but in this case it comes not so much from enemies as those who claim to be with us . . . Good Lord, deliver us from our friends!"

Bloomer found that she and other Iowan officers of the Woman's State Suffrage Society were no longer welcome in state suffrage circles. Disillusioned, she focused her in-person energies on temperance. Her writing activities, however, focused on women's rights after that. Even so, the Woodhull debacle returned to torment her in 1887. When Anthony and Stanton asked Bloomer to write the history of Iowa's suffrage movement for their multivolume history, Stanton rewrote Bloomer's article before publication, taking out the controversy. "Our little dissensions are of little count in the grand onward march," Stanton explained. But Bloomer was listed as the article's author. Readers blamed Bloomer again, this time for trying to "cover up" Iowa's free love scandal.

Bloomer spent the later years of her life caring for children that she and Dexter adopted. She continued to write and serve on church committees. She clipped newspaper articles of interest, keeping abreast of current events to sharpen her printed observations. She died of heart failure on December 30, 1894.

Thirteen years earlier, in 1881, Bloomer had been hurt when Anthony's first volume of the *History of Woman Suffrage* appeared, and *The Lily* was only mentioned in a footnote. Reverend Eugene J. Babcock, who delivered Bloomer's memorial sermon in January 1895, called such contemporary oversights, "the lot of the pioneer." New young suffragists, he said, could not know what the world was like before Bloomer's accomplishments.

Succeeding generations may not always understand Bloomer's obstacles, but they remember her name.

Chronology

MAY 27, 1818	Amelia Jenks born in Homer, New York
1840	marries Dexter Bloomer
1848	attends Seneca Falls Woman's Rights Convention

1849	begins publishing *The Lily* as a "temperance only" paper; becomes Seneca Falls deputy postmistress under Dexter Bloomer
1850	writes first non-temperance, women's rights editorial
1851	writes about "Turkish Dress" in *The Lily*; adopts fashion, which is then nicknamed for Bloomer
1852	makes first public speech; begins speaking career and proclaims *The Lily* "Devoted to the Interests of Woman"
1854	moves *The Lily* to Mount Vernon, Ohio, where she becomes Dexter's assistant editor on temperance paper; hires women typesetters; negotiates subsequent strike
1855	moves to Council Bluffs, Iowa; sells *The Lily*; becomes first Iowa resident to speak on women's rights
1856	addresses Nebraska legislature on woman suffrage
1866	named vice president for Iowa of the American Equal Rights Association (AERA), later the National Woman Suffrage Association (NWSA)
1870	elected Council Bluffs Suffrage Society's first president and first vice president of new Iowa Woman's State Suffrage Society; speaks at state capital rally
1871	elected state suffrage society president; renounces "free love," but not strongly enough to suit conservative suffrage faction

| 1872 | Iowa Suffrage Bill defeated; Bloomer's stand on free love blamed |
| DECEMBER 30, 1894 | Amelia Jenks Bloomer dies |

Further Reading

Bloomer, D. C. *The Life and Writings of Amelia Bloomer*. Boston: Arena Publishing Company, 1895. Reprinted New York: Schocken, 1975. Dexter Bloomer's loving look at his wife's life. Avoids unpleasant details, but it offers glimpses of Bloomer's personality and family life. Adult book; easy reading.

Coon, Anne C., editor. *Hear Me Patiently: The Reform Speeches of Amelia Jenks Bloomer*. Westport, Conn.: Greenwood Press, 1994. A brief biography prefaces complete or near complete texts of Bloomer's speeches. Each speech is introduced with when, where, and why it was given. Bloomer's humor and logic speak for themselves, though her old-fashioned formality makes the reading moderately difficult.

Noun, Louise. "Amelia Bloomer, A Biography: The Lily of Seneca Falls (Part One) and The Suffragist of Council Bluffs (Part Two)," *The Annals of Iowa*, vols. 47 and 48. Iowa City, Iowa: Iowa State Historical Department, 1985. An objective, detailed overview of Bloomer's life. Adult reading level.

————. *Strong-Minded Women: The Emergence of the Woman Suffrage Movement in Iowa*. Ames, Iowa: Iowa State University Press, 1969. Includes all sides, from the famous Bloomer to the infamous Victoria Woodhull. Written in a moderately difficult formal style, reminiscent of the way Bloomer and her contemporaries wrote.

MARY CHURCH TERRELL

(1863 – 1954)

Mary Church Terrell sat in the banker's office, explaining why she'd traveled from Washington, D.C. The War Camp Community Service, she told him, would provide public parks and gyms, recreation, and education for black families in the segregated South. African-American men who had just served in World War I needed those services, and so did black women, who often supported their families. Terrell wasn't asking for money, just local support.

The businessman could tell from Terrell's speech that she wasn't southern. He thought she was well meaning but ill informed. He explained, "Black girls are so bad on general principles, it's useless to try to improve them."

Sadly, Terrell knew what he was talking about. Stories of black housekeepers seduced by their white employers were common. Terrell wondered if the banker knew those housekeepers were

Mary Church Terrell's parents, two former slaves with business savvy, gave their children every privilege money could buy. This picture of Terrell as a student at Oberlin College is proof. (Oberlin College Archives, Oberlin, Ohio)

threatened with unemployment or worse if they refused. Her own black grandmother and white grandfather were examples. Yet it was black women who were branded as "bad," not their white pursuers.

Terrell guessed that this banker, like some other white Americans, didn't believe she was African American. Having never met a black who was well spoken and well dressed, he'd assumed Mary

Church Terrell was from a foreign country—though certainly not one in Africa.

Terrell returned to her campaign. Blacks might improve with opportunities, she argued. The banker cut her off. "I am not opposed to Niggers," he said, "but I want a Nigger to stay in his place."

Mary Eliza Church was born September 23, 1863, in Memphis, Tennessee. Her father, Robert Reed Church, was fast becoming one of America's wealthiest black men as a saloonkeeper, banker, and real estate dealer. Mary's mother, Louisa Ayers Church, was a popular dressmaker and landowner, who catered to what Mary once called "the elite of Memphis." Both former slaves had ambition and business sense.

But Robert and Louise Church divorced, which was considered disgraceful in the 1870s. Sociable, fashion-conscious young Mary was embarrassed that her parents broke their vows. But the Churches continued to share a strong commitment to provide Mary and her young brother with generous opportunities.

Later in her life, Mary Church Terrell would say, "Colored women are the only group in this country who have two heavy handicaps to overcome, that of race as well as that of sex." But Terrell had little inkling of these "handicaps" when she was a child.

Six-year-old Mary began living with a family in Yellow Springs, Ohio, when her mother enrolled her in the experimental Model School at Antioch College there. Mary stayed on when her parents agreed that Yellow Springs public schools would be better than Memphis schools for a bright young black person. Her parents hired a private German tutor for Mary and bought her "everything the hearts of children could desire." Surrounded by privilege, Mary was in elementary school, reading about the Civil War with her class, before she realized that her family—her mother, her father, the Hunsters with whom she boarded—were the people for whom the Civil War was fought. They were the "Negroes" in the history book. And Mary was one of them, too.

She felt stigmatized for a time. Yet in the safety of school, where Mary sang in the choir, played the organ, wore the fashionable dresses her mother sent, and tried not to get in trouble for talking in class, that part of history sometimes seemed far away.

Mary Church attended public high school in Oberlin, Ohio, which had accepted its first black students in 1835. Her 1879 senior preparatory paper, written at age 16, was entitled "Should an Amendment to the Constitution Allowing Women the Ballot be Adopted?" In her paper, Church observed that the rule that home was the "women's sphere" didn't seem to apply when sons needed college money and daughters were asked to earn it. She began to discover that she had an advantage when arguing for women's rights. White suffragists were often sharply criticized for comparing a woman's lot to a slave's. Few people questioned Church's right to do so, even though she had been raised with advantages uncommon to any race.

Church attended Oberlin College, where she participated in the debate team and literary societies that had been closed to Lucy Stone 45 years before. After Church's 1884 graduation, she moved into the Memphis home her father built for her. "He was able and willing to support me" in the manner of southern gentry, Church said. "He did not understand why I wanted to teach or do any kind of work." But she could not shake the feeling that "it was wrong for me to remain idle there."

Church "left home and ran the risk of permanently alienating my father from myself to engage in the work which his money had prepared me to do." She accepted a teaching post at Wilberforce University in Xenia, Ohio, in 1885. Her father didn't speak to her for a year. Two years later, Church joined the foreign language department of the Preparatory School for Colored Youth in Washington, D.C. She was assistant to Latin instructor Robert Heberton Terrell, a pioneering black graduate of Harvard University. Church and Terrell's students eagerly studied the obvious attraction between the two well-bred adults.

Despite the growing friendship, Church's love of languages led her to continue her studies abroad for Oberlin credit. In 1888, 25-year-old Church went to Paris. Funded by her father, she attended a private school for girls and boarded with a local family. She followed the same pattern in Germany and Italy, becoming fluent in three languages in two years. She also learned a lot about America while abroad.

More than once, Church's hostesses came to her, distressed that another American had threatened to leave the boardinghouse if "the Negress" stayed. The landlady seldom understood what the problem was. Church tried to anticipate such incidents. "At what I considered the opportune time, I always told people with whom I boarded how I am classified in the United States," she said. Church sometimes compared America's race prejudice with anti-Jewish sentiments found overseas. But Europeans didn't seem to understand bias against skin color. African Americans often moved overseas for that reason. Church considered that option herself. But as she kept talking with people abroad, Church became convinced that the only way to fight racism was to confront it.

Church returned to the United States in 1890 with a master's degree from Oberlin. Reappointed by the same high school, she happily renewed her friendship with Robert Terrell. She even confessed to him some of her less ladylike qualities: She'd attended a woman suffrage meeting, she said, and stood to proclaim herself a believer in the cause.

"In the early 1890s, it required a great deal of courage for a woman publicly to acknowledge before an audience that she believed in suffrage for her sex," Church explained later. Suffragist Victoria Woodhull's sex scandal had made the cause of women's rights lose respect in the public eye.

But, Church said, "I forced myself to stand up" as a woman suffragist. Robert Terrell laughed at the news, saying she'd never catch a husband that way. When Church retorted she wouldn't marry a non-suffragist, Terrell revealed his true feelings, a statement he later made in public. "I have contempt I cannot name," he said, "for the man who would demand rights for himself that he is not willing to grant everyone else."

Church and Terrell were married in October 1891. The next year, chilling headlines disrupted Mary Church Terrell's new domestic life. Tom Moss, a childhood friend, had been lynched in Memphis.

Unlike other race-related murders, Moss's death became famous when journalist Ida B. Wells publicized the story. Public reaction was strong, as was Terrell's personal response. Her own father had almost died at the hands of Memphis lynchers years before. That beating had left Robert Church physically and emotionally scarred. His daughter knew those scars well.

Terrell wanted to work to make a difference. Her husband, employed at the time in the auditors office of the U.S. Treasury, agreed. When so few black women had been fortunate enough to complete college, he told her, "it would be a shame for any of them to refuse any service it was in their power to give." Robert would continue to urge Mary to public service, even when he became a municipal judge in the District of Columbia and was under the public's watchful eye.

The year of Moss's lynching, Terrell helped found the Colored Women's League (CWL) of Washington, a group dedicated to achieving equal rights for blacks. Some small steps used to achieve this huge goal included local evening school for adults and day care for working mothers' children. Nationally, the league worked for woman suffrage. After all, stopping lynching was a matter of law, and laws could only be changed by ballot.

As chairman of the CWL's educational committee, Terrell taught English literature and German classes for no pay. But even when she wasn't in a classroom, Terrell was teaching. In 1894, she was named head of the Washington department of *Woman's Era* magazine in which she reported on black women's accomplishments in the nation's capital. Over the years, she would write for many national publications. In 1895, she became the first black woman to be named to the District of Columbia Public School Board of Trustees. Terrell launched an educational policy that included black history. Terrell knew from experience that young African Americans could benefit from strong role models. But she also believed that "the only way to 'solve the [race] problem' is to appeal to the sense of justice in the white youth of America."

In 1896, the Colored Women's League joined with other black women's groups to form the National Association of Colored Women (NACW). Terrell was elected its first national president.

She accepted, hoping the NACW would "proclaim to the world that the women of our race have become partners in the great firm of progress and reform."

Under Terrell's guidance, the NACW sponsored kindergartens, day care centers, training schools, mother's clubs, and even orphanages. Terrell wanted to prove that African Americans lacked opportunity, not intelligence.

Terrell believed in displaying how an educated woman could look and act. Despite her wealth, she never lost concern for less fortunate women. (Oberlin College Archives, Oberlin, Ohio)

Robert Terrell suggested that Mary might change the public's perception even more profoundly by giving public speeches. Some of the couple's friends "were so shocked and horrified" at the idea "that words simply failed them," Mary Church Terrell said. Terrell herself was unsure of her skills, and even of her desire to perform. Robert "almost forced me to accept the first [speaking] invitations" by convincing her that, "through the medium of the lecture platform, I would have a better chance of engaging in the work I had always wanted to do than by employing any other method."

Speaking would challenge Terrell throughout her career. Every speech was memorized; she used no notes. The easy parts often came first. Terrell loved to speak of black women's accomplishments, proving ability had nothing to do with race or gender. What followed was seldom as easy. She would carefully cite documented cases of African Americans who had suffered mistreatment and injustice. On one occasion, she said, "My address consumed 50 minutes of which about one minute and a half perhaps, certainly not more, was consumed in referring to the recent riot in St. Louis." Even so, some newspapers described her speeches as "bitter."

"No matter what I say," she wrote in 1940, "I shall be accused either of 'whining' too much or boasting too much."

But most media responded as Terrell hoped they would. One said Terrell's "whole discourse was lacking in all efforts at bloodcurdling and blood-boiling effects. She fired no pyrotechnics." Terrell knew that blaming white audiences would not inspire them to change.

Terrell's initial appearances were so well received that she was hired by the Slayton Lyceum Bureau, an agency that booked her around the country at large gatherings with famous speakers such as William Jennings Bryan. She was paid $15 to $25 a lecture, plus all expenses—quite a bit of money at that time.

In 1898, Susan B. Anthony responded to Terrell's request that the National American Woman Suffrage Association (NAWSA) consider the problems of black women. Anthony asked Terrell to address NAWSA's national convention. Anthony was "thrilled" with Terrell's speech on "The Progress and Problems of Colored Women." In 1900, Terrell again addressed NAWSA's national convention, this time on "The Justice of Woman Suffrage." On this occasion

Terrell's words seemed to focus more on gender than race. But her presence alone, dark skinned in a sea of white, reminded listeners that other African Americans waited for America to keep its promise of opportunity.

The birth of two daughters strengthened Terrell's resolve to help the United States live up to that pledge. Terrell's mother and hired help cared for the children when Terrell was off speaking. When the girls were older, they sometimes traveled with Terrell. Her children attended public school, and Terrell resumed her membership on the Washington, D.C., school board in 1906. This school service shows practical ways in which she tried to improve the world. Though raised in a sheltered manner, she didn't shelter her own children.

Terrell paid attention to educational trends, especially for African Americans. She and her husband both believed Booker T. Washington's new trade schools could help blacks become more self-sufficient as individuals and as a community. The Terrells also supported the work of another black reformer, W. E. B. Du Bois, who encouraged black colleges and academic studies. Many educators saw Du Bois and Washington as opposites. But Terrell supported both. She just wanted African Americans to have choices. In the end, black leaders agreed. Du Bois himself encouraged Terrell to become a founding member of the National Association for the Advancement of Colored People (NAACP) in 1909.

The necessity of the NAACP became clear when the United States joined World War I and needed civilian workers. Despite highly desirable skills in multiple foreign languages, Terrell was hired as a typist. When an official noticed her working among white women, she was reassigned to a less skilled group. Terrell finally quit

*T*he injustice involved in denying woman the suffrage is not confined to the disenfranchised sex alone, but extends to the nation as well, in that it is deprived of the excellent service which woman might render.

—Mary Church Terrell

when yet another official assigned black workers a separate, distant restroom. She then joined the War Camp Community Service.

In 1919, Terrell was thrilled to have the chance to promote "the advancement of colored people" internationally. She addressed the International League for Peace and Freedom in Zurich, representing the International Congress of Women, a group of women from around the world who gathered during the post–World War I treaty conference. They hoped, as women, to contribute to world affairs and the peace process. Yet even here, Terrell was the only person of color.

As the conference got under way, Terrell had a more chilling realization: English was not the conference's universal language. Terrell's speech, "The Contributions and Problems of Blacks in the United States," ought to be translated—and delivered—in German, the host city's tongue. Terrell worked frantically to translate her talk in the hours before she was scheduled to speak. Newspaper headlines around the world showered praise on the only woman to deliver her address in three languages—German, English, and French—and brought attention to Terrell's resolution for international equal rights regardless of race, color, or creed.

Back home, Terrell found the fight for women's rights dividing suffragists. She had long worked with NAWSA, sharing "a delightful, helpful friendship" with its leader, Susan B. Anthony. But Terrell also supported Alice Paul, whose National Women's Party (NWP) picketed the White House, a tactic denounced by NAWSA. Terrell joined the picket with her daughter and even defended Paul against charges of racism when Paul refused to address any cause but woman suffrage.

Terrell herself promoted voting by women long after the 19th Amendment took effect in 1920. That year, Terrell became the president of the Women's Republican League. She was appointed director of work among women of color by the National Republican Committee. With these groups, Terrell tried to bolster party awareness to the needs of black women. Party responsiveness was rewarded by encouraging women to get out and vote Republican. "If we do not use the franchise, we shall give our enemies a stick with which to break our heads, and we shall not be able to live down the reproach of our indifference for 100 years," Terrell told women. "Hold meetings! Every time you meet a woman, talk to her about going to the polls to vote."

Traveling the country for this work, Terrell often encountered "Jim Crow" laws and customs, which forced people of color to use different transportation, rest rooms, restaurants, and hotels from whites. More than once, Terrell ached to challenge those laws in court. Friends begged her not to. Legal action could damage her effectiveness, they warned, or worse still, her husband's in his job as a judge.

Terrell sometimes regretted not fighting back. But she kept "rendering any service it was in her power to give." In the years after Robert Terrell's death in 1925, Mary Church Terrell campaigned for Ruth Hanna McCormick's run for the Illinois Senate. She was the Republican National Committee's eastern director of work among colored women in 1932. In July 1937, Terrell was the featured, closing-night speaker at the International Assembly of the World Fellowship of Faiths in London.

Terrell wrote her autobiography, *A Colored Woman in a White World*, in 1940. A *Current Biography* reviewer remarked, "There is not much in it to indicate that, despite her abilities and good intentions, she has any great understanding of the economic as well as the social angles of the race-prejudice problem, nor does she have many suggestions as to what, by legislation or otherwise, can be done about it."

Terrell spent her last years looking for those answers. In 1949, she became chair of the Coordinating Committee for the Enforcement of District of Columbia Anti-Discrimination Laws. Terrell was finally fighting Jim Crow. At the age of 87, Terrell led the picket of a segregated Kresge's (a dime store chain) lunch counter in the nation's capital. Two years later, in 1952, the Kresge's manager finally spoke with Terrell—and escorted her to the lunch counter for coffee and a piece of pie.

During these later years, Terrell also lobbied Congress for an antilynching bill, a black national monument, and the legalization of interracial marriage. One of her last crusades was on behalf of a black sharecropper who was sentenced to death for killing a white man in self-defense. The case was won five years after Terrell's death. Mary Church Terrell died on July 24, 1954, at her summer home in Annapolis, Maryland. A Washington, D.C., school is named in her honor, as are many black women's clubs.

"My lot might have been much harder, I must confess," she wrote in her autobiography. "I cannot help wondering sometimes what I might have become and might have done if I had lived in a country which had not circumscribed and handicapped me on account of my race, but had allowed me to reach any height I was able to attain." But Terrell knew that handicaps can force people to be more than they dreamed possible, for she also said, "Holding human beings in slavery seems to have been part of the divine plan to bring out the best there is in them."

Chronology

SEPTEMBER 23, 1863	Mary Eliza Church born in Memphis, Tennessee
1869	attends experimental Model School at Antioch College
1884	graduates from Oberlin College
1885	begins teaching career at Wilberforce University in Xenia, Ohio
1888	travels to Europe; studies German, French, and Italian
1890	returns to United States; receives master's degree from Oberlin College
1891	marries Robert Heberton Terrell
1892	cofounds the Colored Women's League (CWL) of Washington
1895	is first black woman appointed to District of Columbia Public School Board of Trustees

1896	National Association of Colored Women (NACW) formed; Terrell elected first president; begins public speaking
1898	addresses national convention of National American Woman Suffrage Association (NAWSA) on "The Progress and Problems of Colored Women"
1909	becomes founding member of the National Association for the Advancement of Colored People (NAACP)
1919	addresses International League for Peace and Freedom in Zurich
1920	becomes president of Women's Republican League and director of work among colored women for National Republican Committee
1940	publishes autobiography, *A Colored Woman in a White World*
1949	chairs Coordinating Committee for the Enforcement of District of Columbia Anti-Discrimination Laws
1950	leads picket of segregated lunch counter in Washington, D.C.
JULY 24, 1954	Mary Church Terrell dies in Annapolis, Maryland

Further Reading

Carney, Jessie, editor. *Epic Lives: 100 Black Women Who Made a Difference.* Detroit: Visible Ink Press, 1993. A short but solid introduction to Terrell.

Dubovoy, Sina. *Civil Rights Leader*. New York: Facts On File, 1997. Contains one chapter on Mary Church Terrell; written for young adults.

Litwack, Leon, and August Meier, editors. *Black Leaders of the 19th Century*. Urbana and Chicago: University of Illinois Press, 1988. Chapter "Mary Church Terrell: Genteel Militant," by Sharon Harley provides a detailed overview of Terrell's life in the context of the world around her. Moderately difficult college text.

McKissack, Pat. *Mary Church Terrell: Leader for Equality*. Hillsdale, N.J.: Enslow Publishers, 1991. A young reader's biography of Terrell.

Terrell, Mary Church. *A Colored Woman in a White World*. National Association of Colored Women's Clubs, Inc., 1968. A thick volume that is hard to get details from. Dates are often obscured in description, and Terrell skirts unpleasant topics. For example, she does not say straightforwardly that her father's former master was her grandfather. Style is conversational yet formal.

"Terrell, Mary Church." *Current Biography*, New York: H.W. Wilson Co., pp. 827–30, 1942. Written shortly after Terrell's autobiography, the authors comment on that book and offer observations of Terrell's contemporaries.

ALICE PAUL

(1885 – 1977)

The nurses were frustrated. Their patient, a stroke victim in her nineties, wasn't eating much. When they tried to reason with her, she refused to eat at all.

They were hopeful when Miss Paul had a visitor. Maybe now she'd be more agreeable. But still she wouldn't eat. The more they asked, the more stubborn she got. The visitor knew why.

Decades ago, Alice Paul had been imprisoned for marching for woman suffrage. She'd protested her arrest with hunger strikes. Her jailers force-fed her: hard, inflexible tubes were worked through her nose into her stomach. Newspapers called the ordeal "bloody and painful." It was also useless: It usually resulted in vomiting. Paul still refused to eat. Her jailers damned themselves with their actions, first in England, then in the United States. Alice Paul's hunger symbolized all women's hunger for justice. Her abuse symbolized women's voicelessness.

Alice Paul, a dedicated pacifist, was often considered dangerous because of her explosive ideas. Her actions attracted crowds, ignited opposition, and humbled a U.S. president. (Smithsonian Institution)

The visitor wasn't sure how much Paul could remember of her past. But, stroke or no stroke, she was still Alice Paul. She would eat when she was ready, and not before.

☆ ☆ ☆

Alice Paul was born on January 11, 1885, in Moorestown, New Jersey. Her father, William Mickle Paul, a businessman, banker, and property owner, died when Alice was just 16. But he knew his oldest child well. Her mother, Tacie Parry Paul, remembered, "Mr. Paul used to say that whenever there was anything hard and disagreeable to do, 'I bank on Alice.'" The Pauls lived in a small Quaker community where Tacie was the clerk of Friends (Quaker) meetings.

"When the Quakers were founded," Alice Paul once explained, "one of their principles was and is equality of the sexes. So I never had any other idea." As a child, Paul went with her mother to Quaker suffrage meetings.

When Paul's father died, he left enough money to support his family for years. So, like her mother, Paul attended Swarthmore College. Classmates later remembered Paul as shy and athletic. She graduated in 1905 as a biology major, which she had chosen before discovering politics her senior year. This new interest sent Paul to the New York School of Philanthropy in 1906 to study sociology. Through sociology, which dissects the origins and functions of society's many relationships, Paul was studying politics. In her spare time, she worked for woman suffrage in New York, gathering voter signatures for a state referendum.

"What a waste of the strength of women to try and convert a majority of men in the state," she said. "I was convinced that the way to do it was through Congress, where there was a smaller group of people to work with."

By 1907, Paul had earned a master's degree in sociology at the University of Pennsylvania. She went to Woodbridge, England, for field work on her doctorate degree. To Paul, and to her professors, social work was meant to be a practical application of sociological theories. But she felt the same frustration in England that she'd felt in New York City. The more experienced Paul became in social work, the more she "knew you couldn't change the situation by social work." In many ways, "the situation" depended on laws. Women had no voice to change the laws because in England, like

America, women couldn't vote. Paul decided woman suffrage could help "change the situation."

The woman suffrage movement in England was unlike anything Paul had seen in America. Led by Emmeline Pankhurst and her daughters, Sylvia and Christabel, British suffragists had begun "wild women" protests in 1905. They sneaked into male political meetings to shout questions, unfurl banners, and be arrested. Paul's participation led some reporters to say the Pankhursts "trained" her in their militant tactics. "Nobody was being trained," Paul protested later. "We were just going in and doing the simplest little things that we were asked to do. You see, the movement was very small in England . . . So I got to know Mrs. Pankhurst."

As Paul became more deeply involved with Pankhurst's group, the Women's Social and Political Union, she was warned of possible imprisonment. Paul later said, "I remember hesitating the longest time" before accepting that risk. But on the day of an important government banquet in 1909, Paul crept into the dining hall's high gallery. She hid there until the evening. When the Lord Mayor rose to speak that night, so did Alice Paul. "I was arrested, of course," she said. This was one of ten times she was arrested in England. Three times, she went to prison. And once, protesting the government's refusal to let women vote or speak, Paul refused to eat. She was force-fed twice daily for four long weeks.

Paul returned to the United States in 1910 where she continued both her suffrage work and her studies. She spoke at that year's National American Woman Suffrage Association's convention on "The English Situation." Two years later, after completing her doctorate degree in sociology at the University of Pennsylvania, Paul was reunited with Lucy Burns, an American she had met in an English jail when both were arrested for protesting.

Paul and Burns knew that, thanks to the Pankhursts, British leaders could not ignore woman suffrage. Newspaper headlines wouldn't let them. Those wild "suffragettes" stoned the prime minister's windows. They set fire to golf courses in the name of woman suffrage. Paul and Burns wanted to rivet American officials' attention in the same way.

They went to the National American Woman Suffrage Association (NAWSA) and proposed forming a committee to lobby congressmen for a national suffrage amendment. "[NAWSA] didn't take the work at all seriously," Paul said later. At the time, NAWSA was focused on state-by-state suffrage referendums. Though Paul and Burns were named president and vice president of NAWSA's new Congressional Committee, the inexperienced women were told they'd have to raise their own funds.

They organized a volunteer network, beginning with former classmates. Then Paul's Congressional Committee began its first bid for national attention: a parade during the celebration of the inauguration of Woodrow Wilson. A parade would be seen by thousands of voters who came to see the new president sworn in, by congressmen who would vote on a suffrage amendment, and by the president, the man with the most influence over Congress. The Congressional Committee had three months. Paul assigned volunteers to contact suffragists around the nation, collect donations, and ask supporters to come march in Washington. The committee couldn't pay travel expenses. However, Paul's hospitality committee found private homes to host marchers, who came by the thousands.

In just weeks, Paul had assembled 8,000 marchers representing states, colleges, occupations, and even several nations. Ten bands, five squadrons of cavalry with chariots, 26 floats, and numerous "tableaux" depicting women's lives all gathered at the nation's capital on March 3, 1913, the day before Wilson's inauguration. Burns marveled at Paul's ability to "make plans on a national scale, and a supplementary power to see that it is done down to the last postage stamp."

The crowd that came to witness the spectacle was estimated at half a million. "There had never been a procession of women for any cause

I *think every reform movement needs people who are full of enthusiasm. It's the first thing you need. I was full of enthusiasm, and I didn't want any lukewarm person around.*

—Alice Paul

under the sun," Paul said. The parade was so enormous that reports of what happened next vary. Paul, marching in the middle with her college, called it "simple overcrowding." Newspapers at the front of the parade called it a riot. Marchers were shoved, taunted, and injured, and 175 ambulances were called. An immediate Senate investigating committee called for charges of police malfeasance. But no matter what anyone said, the parade got people talking. Woman suffrage crashed into the headlines and stayed, which was exactly what Paul had wanted. Within days, her lobbyists presented the suffrage cause to congressmen. By summer, both houses of Congress discussed woman suffrage for the first time in 35 years.

Paul continued to create ways to keep people talking. Her congressional group began publishing its own weekly newspaper, *The Suffragist*. When it debuted in November 1913, Paul's philosophy was boldly stated: "Until women vote, every piece of legislation undertaken by the administration is an act of injustice to them. All laws affect the interests of women." In a December *Suffragist*, Lucy Burns outlined the Congressional Committee's next plan. They would campaign against the party in power, the Democrats, in the next election. Burns and Paul had seen British suffragists fault the head party for suffrage policy. They resolved to oppose Wilson's Democratic party until American suffrage policy changed.

> I*t is not a war of women against men, for the men are helping loyally, but a war of women and men together against the politicians.*
>
> —Alice Paul

NAWSA members were appalled. Democratic allies would be lost by such tactics. Paul insisted, "Whoever was elected from a suffrage state [a state that already had suffrage] was going to be pro-suffrage in Congress anyway, whether he was Republican or Democrat." But NAWSA wouldn't listen. Paul's committee was expelled. The group immediately began preparing for the 1914 election as an independent body called the Congressional Union (CU).

Paul's plan was to "use the nearly 4 million votes that we have [in states with woman suffrage] to win the vote for the rest of the women in the country." She assigned organizers to each of the nine suffrage states. She asked these women to undergo primitive living conditions, bad roads, and isolation, even pay their own expenses. But more than one suffragist "found it impossible to say no to Miss Paul," as historian Inez Haynes Irwin wrote. Suffragist Doris Stevens explained that "if [Paul] has demanded the ultimate of her followers, she has given it herself."

Less than half of the Democratic candidates in 1914 were elected. Paul and the Congressional Union took credit for the losses and rejoiced that "suffragists can actually affect the results of a national election." But Carrie Chapman Catt, the newly elected president of NAWSA, wanted to prove that women would bring higher morality to politics. Paul's aggressive tactics were undoing those arguments. So Catt offered Paul the chance to reunite the Congressional Union and NAWSA. If Paul would give up attacking the Democrats, Catt promised her group would resume supporting a federal amendment.

Paul, confident in her 4,500 members, their weekly newspaper, and their ability to raise funds, did not agree. She was already working on a new plan. In April 1916, just as the U.S. presidential candidates began campaigning, Paul proposed that the Congressional Union branch out into a political party, the National Woman's Party (NWP). The resulting party did not endorse any candidate, only woman suffrage. Even so, the NWP made the other parties nervous. They knew that women's votes could swing the election.

For the first time ever, both parties included support for woman suffrage in their platforms. The election was one of the closest in U.S. history. The Democratic slogan for Wilson's reelection, "He kept us out of war," was countered by the NWP's, "He kept us out of suffrage." As a young professor, Wilson had discouraged higher education for women. Later, as a politician, he alternately dismissed suffrage as a state's rights question or claimed he was helpless without party approval. Yet Wilson would have lost without women: 10 of the 12 suffrage states voted for his peace promise, giving Wilson 277 electoral votes to Republican candidate Charles Evans Hughes's 254.

Although Wilson was elected, the NWP still succeeded. Suffrage, according to the *San Francisco Examiner*, was no longer "a western vagary. Nothing that has 2 million votes is ever vague to the politicians."

Unless the politician was Wilson. Two months later, the president spoke to a group of suffragists and ignored women's contributions to his campaign. The next day, January 10, 1917, women carrying banners began picketing the White House. "Mister President—What Will You Do for Woman Suffrage?" their flags read.

For the next 18 months, suffragists from around the country traveled to Washington, D.C., to join the march. Many who couldn't attend sent supportive letters or money. Organizing it all was Paul. Newspapers loved Paul's "Theme Days," when marchers all hailed from a certain state, college, or profession. Even Wilson and the White House guards would smile and wave when passing.

But a patriotic wave of criticism crashed down on the picketers when America went to war April 6, 1917. The NWP did not support

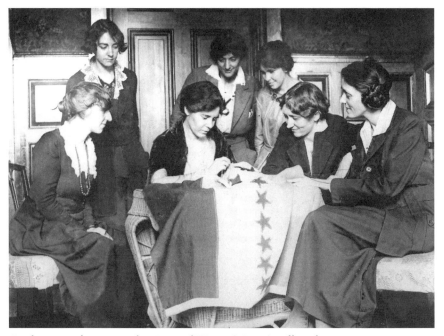

Paul sews another star on the National Women's Party's suffrage banner in 1917, counting the number of states that had granted women the right to vote. (Smithsonian Institution)

the war and would not stop working for suffrage. "If we had universal suffrage throughout the world," Paul said years later, "we might not even have wars."

The picketers began using the war to make points. Wilson had asked America and its allies to "make the world safe for democracy." On June 20, 1917, Russian delegates visiting the White House passed a banner reading, "We women of America tell you that America is not a democracy," and asking Russia to withhold diplomatic relations with America.

Two days later, Lucy Burns and another picketer were arrested for "obstruction of traffic." Paul and others who refilled the picket line knew the charges were false; their actions were protected by local law. But by June 26, there had been 29 arrests.

On June 27, six women came to trial. They refused $25 fines, instead opting for three headline-grabbing days in jail. As new protesters came to trial, sentences got stiffer. By July 14, sentences for suffrage arrests rose to 60 days in Virginia's harrowing Occoquan Workhouse.

The jailed women's lawyer accused Wilson of breaking his campaign promise for suffrage. The president quickly pardoned all suffrage prisoners. "The President can pardon us again if we are arrested on Monday," Paul said. The picketing went on. Paul was arrested on October 20.

Paul's seven-month sentence was the longest given to any suffrage prisoner. She had heard other prisoners' grisly reports of unclean cells, rancid food, parasites, and police brutality. It was all true. When Paul arrived, she broke her cell window with a bowl, because she was unable to breathe the putrid air. Ten days later, she protested with a hunger strike. Force feeding began a week later.

Paul's jailers isolated her, then dumped her in the prison psychiatric ward. "I think," she said later, "the government's strategy was to discredit me. That the other leaders of the Woman's Party would say, well, we had better sort of disown this crazy person. But they didn't." Neither did Dudley Field Malone, Paul's frantic lawyer. He couldn't locate her for an entire month, as prison officials wouldn't reveal where she was.

> I *feel very strongly that if you are going to do anything, you have to take one thing and do it. You can't try lots and lots of reforms and get them all mixed up together.*
>
> —Alice Paul

Paul was alone, questioned, examined, wakened every hour through the night, surrounded by insane inmates and inspectors hoping to commit her. But the truth was reaching the public. On November 10, 1917, the NWP sent out a train called "The Prison Special." Released suffrage prisoners, wearing their prison uniforms, told of the horrific conditions.

Malone finally found Paul on November 20 and rushed her to a regular hospital. One week later, Paul and all suffrage prisoners were released, and the president endorsed a New York State suffrage bill. Within weeks, he openly supported the Anthony Amendment for full woman suffrage. But Paul would believe his support when she saw results. Until then, picketing resumed. Wilson urged individual members of the House and Senate to vote for the 19th Amendment, but it kept losing by the smallest of margins. Paul began burning Wilson's speeches in public. Then in October 1918, Wilson pleaded for woman suffrage as a necessary war measure. Paul called that speech to Congress "magnificent."

The House and Senate both passed the bill in less than a year. By August 18, 1920, 36 states had ratified the proposed amendment. "We thought we never would get that last state," Paul said. "And, you know, President Wilson really got it for us." She had spoken highly of the president even during their stormiest days, and she spoke highly of him till she died.

The National Woman's Party called what might be its final convention in February 1921. Members voted on whether to disband the group or choose a new focus. According to Paul, the women moved to continue because "we can't take out the little slip of paper, the ballot, and give that to our children. We want something to eat, something they can grow strong on." To Paul, that something was equal rights. The group voted to work toward a constitutional Equal

Paul retired to her hometown of Moorestown, New Jersey, before her death at age 92 in 1977. (Smithsonian Institution)

Rights Amendment, the ERA. Years later, Paul would say, "I have never doubted that equal rights was the right direction. Most reforms, most problems are complicated. But to me there is nothing complicated about ordinary equality. Which is a nice thing about our campaign. It really is true, at least to my mind, that only good will come to everybody with equality. . . . It seems to me it is not our problem how women use their equality or how men use their equality."

Soon, Paul went back to school. "I could be more useful to the campaign if I knew more about the law," she said later. In 1922, she received her Bachelor of Laws degree from Washington College of Law. In 1927 and 1928, she earned master's and doctorate law degrees from American University.

The move proved farsighted. As early as 1923, when Paul first wrote the ERA and presented it to Congress, other women's groups opposed it on the grounds that "equality" would mean no work regulations for unskilled female workers. Yet Paul's Equal Rights Amendment was simple and clear: "Equality of rights under the law shall not be denied or abridged by the United States or by any State on account of sex."

Paul expanded her work for equal rights in the 1930s. She served on various national and international groups before forming the World Women's Party in 1939. As its president, she lived for two years in Geneva, Switzerland, where the group was headquartered. She encouraged an Equal Rights Treaty and a World Code of Law. This goal began to be realized in 1945 when gender equality was written into the preamble of the United Nations Charter, thanks in large part to Paul.

To Paul, equal rights was more than just women's rights. "You can't have peace in a world in which some women or some men or some nations are at different stages of development," she said.

Paul focused on equal rights for the rest of her life, nationally and internationally. In 1972, at age 87, Paul finally gave up living in the U.S. capital and moved to a Connecticut cottage. She continued to lobby for the ERA by telephone until she had a stroke in 1974. She then moved into a Quaker nursing home in Moorestown, New Jersey, the town where she was born. Alice Paul died there on July 9, 1977, just as the United States seemed close to ratifying the ERA.[*] In one of her last interviews, Paul was asked what she would work toward after the ERA passed.

Paul listened to the words of the ERA before answering. "It sounds to me," she said, "kind of complete."

---

[*] As of 1998, the ERA had not passed.

Chronology

JANUARY 11, 1885	Alice Paul born in Moorestown, New Jersey
1905	graduates from Swarthmore College
1907	earns master's degree from University of Pennsylvania; studies in England

1908–1909	participates in Pankhurst protests
1910	returns to United States to continue studies at University of Pennsylvania
1912	earns Ph.D. in sociology; becomes chair of the Congressional Committee (CC) of the National American Woman Suffrage Association (NAWSA)
1913	organizes massive suffrage parade and gains national attention; *The Suffragist* begins publication; CC becomes Congressional Union (CU); works for 19th Amendment
1916	National Woman's Party (NWP) formed
JANUARY 1917	Paul begins White House picket for suffrage
MARCH 1917	CU merges into NWP
JUNE 1917	first picket arrests
SEPTEMBER 1917	reports of mistreatment of suffrage prisoners
OCTOBER 1917	Paul is arrested; begins hunger strike 10 days later
NOVEMBER 1917	all suffrage prisoners released
1920	19th Amendment for woman suffrage ratified
1921	NWP focus becomes Equal Rights Amendment (ERA)
1922	Paul earns bachelor's degree from Washington College of Law
1923	drafts and presents ERA to Congress

1927 AND 1928	earns advanced law degrees from American University
1939	founds World Women's Party for international gender equality
1945	helps draft ERA into preamble of United Nations charter
JULY 9, 1977	Alice Paul dies in Moorestown, New Jersey

Further Reading

Faber, Doris. *Petticoat Politics.* New York: Lothrop, Lee & Shepard Co, 1967. A detailed young adult retelling of the suffrage movement from Seneca Falls to the 19th Amendment. Includes background information on Britain's Pankhursts. A rare source that does not make either Paul or Carrie Chapman Catt a villain. Lots of documented quotes, with plenty of author explanations on period attitudes.

Gallagher, Robert S. "I was arrested, of course . . ." *American Heritage: The Magazine of History,* vol. XXV, no. 2, February 1974. Accessible interview with Paul shortly before her stroke, which includes her personal insights about her past and the women's movement of the 1970s.

Lunardini, Christine A. *From Equal Rights to Equal Suffrage: Alice Paul and the National Women's Party, 1910–1928.* New York: New York University Press, 1986. A detailed account of Paul's involvement in the struggle for the 19th Amendment. This adult book focuses on the politics Paul encountered during these years, with few insights to Paul's personality.

Wedemeyer, Lee. "A Salute to Originator of ERA in 1923," *New York Times,* January 10, 1977. One of Paul's last interviews includes her perspectives on the past and a description of Paul's appearance and actions during her final days.

CARRIE CHAPMAN CATT

(1859–1947)

Carrie Lane got still another invitation to go walking on Saturday. She'd never received so many offers to go to the college promenade. For 90 precious minutes each week, couples dressed in their best walked outdoors, unchaperoned. Coeducational schools monitored students carefully in 1877. That's why Iowa State College's afternoon walk was anticipated all week.

Lane thought she must have 50 invitations this week—and she knew why. Before Lane came, the college literary society had a rule that women couldn't speak at meetings. While the other (male) students debated, defended, and exchanged ideas, the women could only read prepared papers.

Lane had broken that rule. She'd enjoyed speaking so much that she wanted to practice. She planned a ladies debate club, but the only available meeting time was during Saturday's "walk." When Lane scheduled the meeting anyway, she was bombarded with invitations.

Lane thought she knew the reason for her sudden appeal. The boys weren't trying to woo her. They were trying to save the walk. Lane

Suffragists feared that widow Carrie Lane Chapman would abandon suffrage work when she married George Catt in 1890. But six years later, when this photograph was taken, Carrie Chapman Catt was still a leader in the national woman suffrage movement. (National 19th Amendment Society)

loved the walk, too. After all, the walk was tradition. But she wanted to start a new, more important tradition. Years later, she found words to describe the struggle.

"Women are not in rebellion against men," she said. "They are in rebellion against worn-out traditions."

☆ ☆ ☆

Carrie Lane was born on January 9, 1859, in Ripon, Wisconsin. Her father, Lucius Lane, moved the family to a farm outside of Charles City, Iowa, by the time his daughter was seven. Carrie's mother, Maria, who had attended a woman's college, preferred the activity of the small Iowa town to isolated Wisconsin. A middle child with two brothers, Carrie later called herself "an ordinary child. What happened to me . . . must have happened to thousands of other ordinary boys and girls in equally ordinary schools and towns." She remembered one "ordinary" episode all her life:

> When I was nearly twelve years old and it was nearing election time, which I had noticed for the first time, I named the kittens after all the candidates. On Election Day, my father drove past the house . . . taking the men to vote. When he returned home, I asked him "Why didn't Mother go to vote?"

Lucius Lane didn't have an answer. Neither did Iowa State College, which didn't allow its female students to speak in public or take part in physical education when Carrie Lane enrolled in 1877. Lane's protests changed those policies before she graduated in 1880, the only woman in a class of 18. She had also polished her debating skills off campus, giving her first public suffrage speech at age 18.

Lane worked in a small law office before becoming a teacher in Mason City, Iowa. Women had opportunities in the Iowa education system: Lane was high school principal after one year and school superintendent after two. But no one was surprised when she resigned. After all, Mason City newspaper editor Leo Chapman had just proposed marriage, and brides in 1885 didn't pursue professions. That is, unless they married someone like Leo Chapman. He rushed his wife's name onto his newspaper's masthead as coeditor and assigned her a new column called "Woman's World."

Carrie Chapman debated women's lives in print: the lack of education and employment for women, different pay for equal work, "silly" fashions, "women's" magazines featuring only "poodles" and stories of romantic "mashes [flirtations]," social disdain toward

> Even anti-suffragists do not stay at home. They come clear out here to Iowa from the East to tell the men not to give women the vote because women's place is in the home.
>
> —Carrie Chapman Catt

unmarried women, the isolation and drudgery of women in their own homes that she believed could be remedied by communal eateries. Her writing was confident, sarcastic, and funny.

Newspaper writers were allowed to report their opinions on the facts back then. But that fall, Leo Chapman's opinion of a local politician resulted in a libel suit. Libel suits were unheard of in 1885 journalism, and both Chapmans panicked. Fearing the jury would be paid to convict him, Leo Chapman sold his paper. The young couple would start over out west.

Carrie Chapman waited in Iowa with her parents while Leo shopped for a San Francisco newspaper. He telegrammed at the end of the summer, but it wasn't the message she expected: Leo Chapman had typhoid fever. He died before she could reach him.

Alone in San Francisco, Carrie Chapman looked for work at newspapers. Although she had experience as a columnist, she was offered a job selling ads. "It was at this time that she met with an experience which was really the turning point in her life," the *Des Moines Register* reported years later. "Meeting men, as she did from day to day, she discovered that women were not given the respect which they rightfully deserved. . . ."

Chapman, so private that she destroyed many personal papers, rarely detailed this "experience." Friend and biographer Mary Peck later learned the young widow had been molested by a newspaper client. The *Register*'s readers knew only that Chapman became "determined to work for the ballot for women, because she felt that they needed it for their own protection."

Chapman left newspaper work, where she no longer had a voice, and began a career as a public speaker. She wrote three speeches, all using current events to support a message of women's rights. After successfully testing the speeches in California churches, Chapman returned to Iowa in 1887.

She moved to Charles City so that her younger brother could live with her while attending high school. For two years she lectured and worked for suffrage with a local group. In October 1889, she attended the Iowa Woman Suffrage Association convention. After presenting a paper, she was promptly elected state secretary. One month later, She was off to 15 Iowa cities, lecturing and organizing suffrage clubs. She represented Iowa around the country, even at the emotional 1890 convention of the National American Woman Suffrage Association (NAWSA). At this, Chapman's first national convention, Lucy Stone and Elizabeth Cady Stanton reunited their factions after 20 years apart.

Chapman continued touring inside Iowa and out. She returned from an 1890 western tour with a surprise that horrified her coworkers: a husband. George Catt had attended Iowa State College at the same time as Chapman. He'd been in San Francisco when she was there, too. Their friendship had grown as her public career did. To the relief and disbelief of Iowa suffragists, George Catt had no intention of asking his wife to abandon her work. "My husband used to say that he was as much a reformer as I," Carrie Catt said later, "but that he couldn't work at reforming and earn a living at the same time . . . what he could do was to earn a living enough for two and free me from all economic burden, and thus I could reform for two. That was our bargain, and we happily understood each other."

Two months after their wedding, Carrie Catt was off to South Dakota to lobby for a state suffrage amendment. NAWSA was hopeful for this campaign. Wyoming had just gained statehood, becoming America's first suffrage state (although women had enjoyed the right to vote in the territory since 1869). Voters in South Dakota could be galvanized by this success.

Catt was sure that South Dakotans wanted woman suffrage. After hard days farming they traveled hours to hear her speak. They shared their food and homes with her, even if the food was watermelon and tea and the home was one room with a blanket hung between beds. But most businessmen didn't want women voting. Liquor makers feared women would outlaw alcohol; industrialists worried women would impose costly safety standards; politicians expected moral matrons to keep them from buying immigrants' votes. Woman suffrage was defeated.

In 1923, writing about the history of the suffrage movement, Catt believed the corruption of politicians and businessmen delayed success. "It was not an antagonistic public sentiment, nor yet an uneducated or indifferent public sentiment—it was the control of public sentiment, the deflecting and the thwarting of public sentiment, through the trading and the trickery, the buying and the selling of American politics . . . combines of interests that systematically fought suffrage with politics and effectively delayed suffrage for years."

Catt didn't like politics, but she had a political goal. She decided that learning to use the political system was the only way to beat it. Catt spent the winter of 1891 with Lucy Stone, an experienced suffrage campaigner. Stone was near death but eager to see the fight for women's rights continue.

Back in Iowa that spring, Catt pioneered suffrage clubs in every county and many towns. She looked "for a trusty *man* in every precinct." After all, only men could vote for suffrage. Men might be more convinced by other men. Catt directed workers to plan suffrage conventions during county fairs, which provided ready-made audiences. She sent speakers to teacher's institutes and to community groups. She created a special "Sunday Speech," for most working folks were only free on Sundays. Catt's talk, "The Bible and Woman Suffrage," was effective with conservatives, she said, and those were the voters suffrage needed. Their support allowed Catt to warn every legislator that "some of his constituents wanted woman suffrage, and if he didn't, he would be defeated."

Catt's tactics were raved about in suffrage circles. NAWSA asked her to repeat her program in Colorado. By avoiding publicity, a state suffrage bill had passed both houses before anti-suffragists had a chance to oppose it. The decision for suffrage was up to Colorado voters now. Catt went to the voters and won. In 1893, Colorado became the second suffrage state.

Catt expanded upon this success with another of Lucy Stone's ideas: She developed a three-year educational course for suffragists. Local clubs would administer the course, which included gathering

ADVERTISEMENT. | ADVERTISEMENT. | ADVERTISEMENT. | ADVERTISEMENT.

TO THE IOWA FARMER!--REMEMBER!

WOMAN SUFFRAGE
MEANS HIGH TAXES

TAX RATE IS BOUND TO INCREASE

The History of Equal Suffrage States is the Story of Taxpayers' Money Wasted---Money Thrown Away in Hysterical Legislation, Useless Commissions, Uncalled for Bond Issues, Increased Election Costs---Taxes are Squandered Because of a Catering of Legislative Interests to the Irresponsible Elements Among Voters. Compare this Government Report:

Non-Suffrage States	Tax per $1,000	Equal Suffrage States	Tax per $1,000
Wisconsin	$11.80	Washington	$31.00
New Hampshire	16.00	Colorado	40.10
Vermont	18.83	Utah	32.60
Missouri	19.00	Wyoming	32.40
Massachusetts	17.30	California	21.50
IOWA	12.04	Idaho	41.50

("Vol. 1, p. 351—Taxation Statistics Census Report.")

TAX RIDDEN CALIFORNIA

During the first four years of Woman Suffrage in California, 1911 to 1915, state taxes were increased from 18 to 36 millions, or 100 per cent increase. The cost of county government is the highest of any state in the Union. Los Angeles alone cost the taxpayers 42 millions. Los Angeles Times says: "10 millions is political plunder."

DO YOU WANT THIS IN IOWA?

COLORADO'S EXPERIENCE

Denver has the highest tax rate of any city of its size in the world—$26.00 for every man, woman and child in the city. Colorado has the highest state tax in the Union. The Denver Post protests that "Public funds are notoriously wasted through useless commissions, and loose political methods."

DO YOU WANT THIS IN IOWA?

TAX CRISIS IN IOWA

Taxpayers of Iowa today are entering a Protest against the Squandering of Public Funds. The Cost of running the State of Iowa has been for the Biennial Periods: Ending June 30, 1895, $3,624,000. Ending June 30, 1914, $11,996,000. Note this Enormous Increase in Taxes with no Increase in Population.

Facing this Critical Situation It Is No Time to Increase State Expenses by adopting Woman Suffrage and assuming Additional Election Expenses of a Million Dollars.

VOTE "NO" ON JUNE 5

The Farmers of Iowa should remember that the granting of Woman Suffrage means the doubling of the city vote in Iowa which has no thought of their interests and does not materially increase the farm vote. "It is not your wife and daughter who will vote, but the women of towns and cities who have easy access to the polls and axes to grind."

YOU, MR. FARMER, MUST PAY THE BILL. CAN YOU AFFORD THIS EXPERIMENT AT THIS TIME?

IOWA ASSOCIATION OPPOSED TO WOMAN SUFFRAGE   DES MOINES, IOWA

THIS ADVERTISEMENT PAID FOR BY POPULAR SUBSCRIPTION AMONG PATRIOTIC IOWANS

Raised in Iowa, Catt collected both support and opposition in her home state, as proven by this 1916 Iowa newspaper ad. The state's women didn't get suffrage until 1919, during the rush to ratify the federal 19th Amendment. (Burling Library, Grinnell College)

CARRIE CHAPMAN CATT

data on women taxpayers. Catt's studies would prove how much American women were taxed, justifying woman suffrage. After all, America was founded on the idea that "taxation without representation is tyranny." Catt's course would teach suffragists how to convince both voters and legislators. "The time has come to cease talking to women," she said, "and invade town meetings and caucuses."

Catt learned to work inside the political system, but she was sometimes frustrated. In her address to the 1901 NAWSA convention, Catt blasted politicians who ignored educated, tax-paying women like her listeners. Instead, votes were given to "the foreigner, the Negro and the Indian. Perilous conditions, seeming to follow from this introduction into the body politic of vast numbers of irresponsible citizens, have made the nation timid" to enfranchise women, she said. For years, Catt advocated voting qualifications, such as requiring voters to have a certain amount of education or property. Such qualifications would keep votes from "irresponsible citizens." To Catt, voting was an earned privilege, not a right of birth. Her anger at being denied this privilege sometimes targeted minorities. Her opinions changed, but over many years. That change began in 1893 at the Chicago World Fair's Congress of Representative Women from All Lands, which was Catt's first real opportunity to meet and talk with people from around the world.

In 1896, Catt spoke, taught, and organized in Idaho, the third victory for woman suffrage. She went on to California, the most intense campaign yet, for the opposition was organized and prepared. California suffrage did not pass. But Catt's leadership shone, even without victory. In 1900, Susan B. Anthony

> Though suffrage would bring with it duties which . . . might be unpleasant . . . is certainly true; but results are now forced upon women which are . . . obnoxious because [they] cannot vote. No one asserts the ballot will bring a paradise to womanhood.
>
> —Carrie Chapman Catt

named Carrie Chapman Catt as the new president of NAWSA.

Catt's vision was expanding by now. She knew how distant politicians affected the lives of ordinary women. She began wondering how the world affected women, and how women affected the world.

Catt compiled the first international study on the status of women in 1902. She sent questionnaires around the world. The contacts made here helped Catt found the International Woman Suffrage Alliance (IWSA) in 1904.

In that same year, George Catt developed stress-induced stomach troubles that demanded a vacation, and Carrie Chapman Catt resigned the NAWSA presidency to travel with him in Europe. She attended the first International Woman Suffrage Alliance conference in Berlin and became its president, a post she could continue by mail from home. But only weeks after coming home, George Catt died. Carrie turned to her closest suffrage friend, Mary Hay. The two were roommates until Hay's death in 1928. Carrie Chapman Catt's will asked to be buried beside Hay.

Soon after her husband's death, Catt's mother and brother died, too. Grief affected her health. She traveled again to rest her body. Instead, she found her despairing spirits rejuvenated by cultures and people overseas. "The only way for you to live was to fill your life so full of work, you could not think of unhappy things," Mary Peck once told her. Even on vacation, Catt was making speeches and organizing women for suffrage.

Catt returned to the United States in 1912, ready to conquer another state. New York suffrage could boost the national campaign with its influential electoral votes. Catt was still at work in New York when she was again elected the president of NAWSA in 1915. She accepted on the condition that Mary Hay, her New York second in command, take over that campaign. NAWSA agreed, and Catt responded with what came to be known as "Mrs. Catt's Winning Plan."

Catt's "Winning Plan" was simple. Instead of focusing entirely on state referendums or a national amendment, Catt proposed pursuing states' rights in the conservative South and an amendment in the liberal North.

The Winning Plan was political, and Catt steeled herself to act politically. Catt called herself a pacifist, but when the United States entered World War I, Catt supported the war. Germany's attacks on U.S. ships had roused a seemingly universal patriotism. If suffragists supported patriotism, she argued, patriots would vote for suffrage. Catt volunteered NAWSA as a national clearinghouse for women's groups serving the war effort. She denounced Alice Paul's wartime suffrage protests. Catt even refused to endorse suffragist Jeannette Rankin, the first woman to serve in the House of Representatives. Catt believed Rankin's congressional vote against the war "set back the cause" of suffrage.

In 1917, three more states added suffrage, and one of them was New York. With New York votes, Congress approved a national suffrage amendment in 1918. But the bill went down in the Senate by one vote. Catt kept her lobbyists in Washington and around the country visiting and telephoning senators and representatives. President Wilson, goaded by the White House protests of suffragist Alice Paul and her headline-grabbing arrests, felt forced to address the issue. Even his own daughters supported suffrage. Wilson invited respectable, patriotic Mrs. Catt to the White House to signal his new approval of women's votes. Again Congress approved the Anthony Amendment, and again the Senate killed it.

World War I ended in 1918, but the suffrage war trudged on. Women only needed a vote or two in the Senate. The new legislature elected in 1918 could give them those votes. Catt's hopes ran so high she helped found the League of Women Voters, an educational group that would prepare women to vote. At last, both houses of Congress approved the bill in 1919.

It was up to the states now, and the race was on. Women wanted to vote for president in the 1920 election. Suffragists began rushing bill after bill through state legislatures to ratify the amendment. A majority of 36 states needed to approve amending the Constitution. The last state, Tennessee, completed the quest in August.

It was over. But Catt, eager to work internationally again, barely stopped to rest. President Wilson was now promoting a League of Nations, and Catt was fascinated. Like suffrage in its early days, the new idea of a world union wasn't popular in America. Catt's support suddenly made her "unpatriotic" in newspaper columns.

Catt was used to being part of a cause that "began more than 100 years ago, and probably will not come to its end for a very long time in the future." In 1925, Catt founded the Committee for the Cause and Cure of War. International contacts kept Catt informed on

Catt was an involved activist until her 1947 death, moving from the cause of suffrage to that of world peace. (Courtesy of League of Women Voters Archives)

conditions abroad, and Catt spread the news in America. Soon after Hitler came into power in Germany, Catt rallied Americans to stop Nazi hate crimes and to take in refugees. She was awarded the American Hebrew medal for promoting understanding between Christians and Jews in 1933. She expanded on that work by giving time and ideas toward establishing the United Nations in 1944.

Catt's final years, interviews, and speeches all focused on the issue of peace. Her views evolved over the years. Catt had been raised with stories of "brutal, treacherous, murderous Indians" which she still believed when she was 35. She was in her sixties before she realized, "We [Caucasians] stole land, whole continents." In 1921, Catt told the Iowa State College graduating class, "You must think internationally. You are members of the human race . . . Let us be a nation with sympathy enough to put war out of the world." After Catt's death on March 9, 1947, at her New York home, her later years of peace were ignored.

In 1995, 75 years after Catt helped win the vote and 48 years after her death, Iowa State College (now Iowa State University) renovated one of its historic buildings. The school honored its famous alumna by naming the site Carrie Chapman Catt Hall. As the dedication was being planned, so were protests.

Some students were offended by Catt's early statements scapegoating foreigners and people of color. To honor such a person was insulting, protesters said. They demanded the building not be named for Catt. Debate went on for years.

Some scholars argued Catt's earlier statements had been taken out of context. It was wrong to apply 1990s political correctness to Catt's bigoted political world, they said. If Catt had made race an issue, they argued, it would have delayed woman suffrage for all colors.

Others pointed to Catt's friendships with noted African Americans like Mary Church Terrell. Terrell wrote in 1940, "Mrs. Carrie Chapman Catt, one of the 12 foremost women in the United States, has demonstrated her freedom from race prejudice and her friendship for me over and over again, ever since I met her at least 30 years ago."

Still others argued that Catt was being held to a standard that apparently didn't apply to men. Buildings named for President

Thomas Jefferson should be renamed too, they contended, because Jefferson owned slaves.

Catt's beliefs about other people evolved as years went by. But another of her beliefs stayed constant. "The chief control of my life is faith in God's eternal law for the evolution of the race," she said. She had "faith that evolution would allow no permanent harm to come to the [human] race through its stupidity and blunders."

Chronology

JANUARY 9, 1859	Carrie Lane born in Ripon, Wisconsin
1880	graduates from Iowa State College
1885	marries newspaper editor Leo Chapman; writes column "Woman's World"
1886	Leo Chapman dies
1889	Carrie Chapman is appointed Iowa Woman Suffrage Association secretary
1890	marries George Catt
1893	helps first successful state suffrage campaign in Colorado
1895	formulates suffrage education program
1900	becomes president of National American Woman Suffrage Association (NAWSA)
1902	sponsors first international study on the status of women
1904	cofounds International Woman Suffrage Alliance
1905	George Catt dies
1911	travels world promoting suffrage and international peace
1915	begins second term as NAWSA president

1919	cofounds League of Women Voters
1920	19th amendment for woman suffrage passes
1925	Catt founds Committee for the Cause and Cure of War
1933	receives American Hebrew medal for educating Americans about Nazi hate crimes
1943	works toward establishment of United Nations
MARCH 9, 1947	Carrie Chapman Catt dies in her New York home

Further Reading

Faber, Doris. *Petticoat Politics.* New York: Lothrop, Lee & Shepard Co, 1967. A detailed young adult retelling of the suffrage movement from Seneca Falls to the 19th Amendment. Lots of documented quotes, with plenty of author explanations on period attitudes. Catt anecdotes in closing chapters.

Noun, Louise. *Strong-Minded Women.* Ames, Iowa: Iowa State University Press, 1969. An overview of the woman's suffrage movement with particular emphasis on Iowa. Basic Catt information concentrated near book's end but sprinkled throughout. Valuable perspective of a big movement in small towns. Formal adult style of moderate difficulty.

Peck, Mary Gray. *Carrie Chapman Catt.* New York: H.W. Wilson Company, 1944. Written by Catt's close friend and admirer, this book contains interesting personal anecdotes but little objectivity. Old-fashioned conversational style, scanty on some dates and journalistic details.

Van Voris, Jacqueline. *Carrie Chapman Catt: A Public Life.* New York: The Feminist Press, 1987. A detailed view of Catt's public life, with many quotes from Catt and her contemporaries. College level, detailed but not hard to follow. Well indexed.

JEANNETTE PICKERING RANKIN

(1880–1973)

After Pearl Harbor was attacked in 1941, President Franklin Roosevelt called an emergency session of Congress to declare war on Japan. Only one representative voted against the president's wishes. "As a woman, I cannot go to war," Representative Jeannette Rankin spoke out, "and I refuse to send anyone else."

Public response was swift and furious. Rankin required a police escort from the House Chamber back to her office. Officers guarded her door as she worked. But police couldn't hold back the crush of enraged mail that hit Rankin's box. She responded personally to every missive.

"What one decides to do in a crisis depends on one's philosophy in life," Rankin wrote to a friend, "and that philosophy cannot be changed by an accident. If one hasn't any philosophy, in crises others make the decision. The most disappointing feature of working for

Montana native Jeannette Pickering Rankin, photographed in 1906, 10 years before she became the United States' first congresswoman (Montana Historical Society)

WOMEN SUFFRAGISTS

a cause is that so few people have a clear philosophy of life. We used to say, in the suffrage movement, that we could trust the woman who believed in suffrage, but we could never trust the woman who just wanted to vote."

Jeannette Pickering Rankin was born on a ranch near Missoula, Montana, on June 11, 1880. Her father, John Rankin, was a rancher and a builder. His second house, in town, showcased Missoula's first central heating and modern bath facilities.

But Jeannette, the oldest of six sisters and a brother, enjoyed the more rugged life on the ranch. Throughout her life, Rankin often chose to live without modern conveniences, such as plumbing and electricity, and to tend to simple needs such as sewing and cooking herself. Her mother, Olive, a former schoolteacher, made sure her children learned domestic skills.

Montana itself was rugged and new. Members of the Native American Nez Perce tribe were still a common sight. Rankin's father said that the Nez Perce were peaceful, yet he'd been called to fight in the "Indian Wars" to keep the tribe from using guns to hunt. The government had been wrong, he said. His daughter remembered the story.

The Rankins sent their children to college. Jeannette Rankin graduated from the University of Montana in 1902 with a degree in biology and a desire to work. But she had no idea what to work at.

Rankin was working as a dressmaker in Montana when her father contracted spotted fever and died in 1904. Rankin's loss was keen. She went to be with her brother, Wellington, who was attending school in Boston. The poverty of the city had a profound impact on Rankin; instead of going home, she went to work in a settlement house in San Francisco. Next, she attended the New York School of Philanthropy to learn more about social work. In 1910, she started working at an orphanage in Spokane, Washington. At the time, newspapers in Washington were full of articles about an upcoming vote on woman suffrage. Rankin, frustrated with the bureaucracy at the orphanage, responded to the idea of suffrage. She wanted a voice, and she wanted to make a difference.

Rankin went to Seattle, Washington. While taking graduate courses at the University of Washington, including a class on public speaking, Rankin joined the Washington Equal Suffrage Association. She brought the social ease of sparsely settled Montana to her work. Rankin didn't mind talking with men in barbershops and bars, places many suffragists were too timid to go. Raised like a son by her father, Rankin joked, asked questions, and listened. And she didn't worry about arguing in a polite way. "You give us the responsibility of raising children," Rankin reminded men who asked why women needed votes, "but we have nothing to say about the laws that affect our children."

Rankin's first political mentors were women experienced at canvasing neighborhoods and organizing local groups and events. Their methods resulted in woman suffrage for Washington State in 1910. Rankin went straight back to Montana to apply what she'd learned to the suffrage campaign starting there. Rankin even added an idea of her own. She asked permission to address the Montana state legislature. No woman had ever done that before.

For the first of many times, Rankin's mother and siblings helped her prepare, then cheered her on when she made her speech to a packed house on February 11, 1911. "At the beginning of this country's history," Rankin said, "men gave their lives for a principle. It was: Taxation without representation is tyranny! Women struggle now for the same principle: 'No taxation without representation!'" Her audience, in the gallery and in the press, responded enthusiastically. The bill missed passage by a small margin, but Rankin received an offer to work for the New York Woman Suffrage Party in May 1911.

New York "loaned" Rankin to California, where workers were needed for the upcoming state suffrage amendment vote. California became suffrage's biggest state victory to date. By 1912, Rankin was the field secretary for the National American Woman Suffrage Association (NAWSA). She traveled, gave speeches to large groups and small, formed suffrage clubs, and lobbied government officials. Rankin met state legislators and U.S. congressmen, the people who made the laws. She talked with the people who worked and voted and obeyed those laws. She heard the differences between what working people wanted and what the government gave them. The differences were obvious in 1914, when Rankin returned to Montana to campaign for a woman suffrage popular vote. Only two months before that election, the first battles of World War I erupted in Europe.

Rankin believed the war was "a commercial war, that none of the idealistic hopes would be carried out, and I was aware of the falseness of much of the propaganda." By convincing voters that universal woman suffrage could better the world and possibly even bring peace, Rankin helped Montana win woman suffrage in 1914.

Rankin was hungry to see woman suffrage in action. In 1915, she took the first of many journeys around the globe. Rankin traveled to New Zealand, where women had voted for 20 years. She took a factory seamstress job to find out how ordinary women lived. To her dismay, she discovered that working conditions for women there were just as bad as those in the United States, despite woman suffrage. But as usual, Rankin just rolled up her sleeves. Years later, she told the *New York Times* that she began working as a private seamstress in New Zealand so that she could talk to customers while she pinned up their hems, convincing them to support better labor laws for women. Again, Rankin's quest was successful.

M*ight it not be that the men who have spent their lives thinking in terms of commercial profit find it hard to adjust themselves to thinking in terms of human needs? Might it not be that a great force that has always been thinking in terms of human needs and that always will think in terms of human needs has not been mobilized? Is it not possible that the women of the country have something of value to give the nation at this time?*

—Jeannette Pickering Rankin

Meeting people, finding out how their lives could be better, then working to make it so—Rankin had found the pattern of work she would pursue for the rest of her life. When she arrived home, Montana was preparing for its first election with women voters. It occurred to Rankin, "We are half of the people, we should be half of the Congress." She decided to run for the U.S. House of Representatives. Years later, she said, "I ran to repay the women of Montana who had worked for suffrage."

Rankin's brother, Wellington, served as her campaign manager. Montana's former suffrage clubs, which Rankin knew so well, were reformed as pro-Rankin Good Government Clubs. Rankin won the Republican nomination by a large margin. Afterward, Montana women of every party helped her campaign. Rankin's platform included national woman suffrage, infant and maternal health care, an eight-hour workday for women, tax law reform, and peace.

On November 6, 1916, Rankin cast her first vote as a newly enfranchised woman of Montana. She voted for herself. So did enough other women and men that Rankin was the only successful Montana Republican candidate. She was the first woman ever elected to the United States Congress and the first woman elected to any national government in the world.

On April 2, 1917, Rankin was the guest of honor at a suffragists' breakfast celebrating her first day in office in Washington, D.C. There were flags and flowers and an open-car parade celebrating the first American woman with a strong voice in government. But trouble surrounded Rankin even then. Conservative Carrie Chapman Catt sat on one side of her at breakfast, radical Alice Paul on the other. Everyone knew the United States was about to enter the war. Paul, like Rankin, was a pacifist and saw suffrage as a step for peace. Catt wanted suffrage, and if suffragists had to support war to get women's votes, Catt would support the war.

Rankin made a happy, historic entry into the House of Representatives, Montana's other representative John Evans on one arm, a bouquet of flowers on the other. Many incumbent congressmen knew Rankin from her days as a lobbyist. Members of the Rankin family watched from the packed gallery. At Rankin's appearance, the crowd erupted into applause.

That evening President Woodrow Wilson announced his intention to go to war. Debate in Congress went on for four days. Catt warned Rankin that a vote against war would be a vote against suffrage. Rankin's brother said that voting against war would show that women didn't understand the complexities of government. Rankin herself knew her single vote would not stop the fighting. She could avoid much political turmoil by just voting "yea."

But, Rankin said, "I felt that the first time the first woman in Congress had a chance to say no to war, she should say it." And that is what Rankin did. Forty-nine other congressmen voted no, as did six senators.

Once war was declared, Rankin was practical about it. The first time she made a speech to the house, she called for equal opportunity for women in jobs, especially in war industry. She promoted Liberty Bonds for the war effort. She even voted for the draft, for she often said, "If they are going to have a war, they ought to take the old men and leave the young men to carry on the race." But she protested a bill that was passed, which imprisoned draft protesters. Rankin also

Rankin, with shovel, is flanked by Belle Fligelman (left), planting a tree on the lawn of the U.S. Capitol during a 1917 Arbor Day ceremony. (Montana Historical Society)

JEANNETTE PICKERING RANKIN

criticized the treatment of Alice Paul and other "unpatriotic" suffragists imprisoned for picketing the White House for suffrage.

President Wilson tried to use war as an excuse to ignore suffrage. But Rankin could not ignore the suffragists she had visited in dirty cells. When they refused to eat, they were force-fed with tubes through the nose. Rankin called for a congressional investigation of their treatment. The public was outraged when reports of the abuse came out. Rankin took advantage of this pro-suffrage sentiment by presenting the Anthony Amendment for woman suffrage to Congress on January 10, 1918. She even took full advantage of the patriotism induced by the war she despised. She said:

> Today as never before, the nation needs its women, needs the work of their hands and their hearts and their minds. Are we now going to refuse these women the opportunity to serve, in the face of their plea, in the face of the nation's great need? . . . The boys at the front know something of the democracy for which they are fighting. These courageous lads who are paying with their lives testified to their sincerity when they sent home their ballots in the New York election and voted two to one in favor of woman suffrage and democracy at home. Can we afford to permit a doubt as to the sincerity of our protestations of democracy?

Four congressmen came from sickbeds, one from his wife's deathbed, to vote for the amendment. The House passed woman suffrage by one vote. Suffrage lost in the Senate by two. The bill would not come to a vote again for two years. By then, Rankin's term was over, and she was not reelected.

Because of Rankin's vote against war, Carrie Chapman Catt urged members of NAWSA to vote for Rankin's opponent in 1918. Montana mine owners lobbied against Rankin because she worked for costly safety regulations in the mining industry. Other people didn't like Rankin because she'd sponsored the first-ever mother and child health bill. Few people were comfortable discussing the topics covered in Rankin's bill: birth control, sexually transmitted diseases, maternal and infant hygiene. But Rankin said, "The Government had always offered instruction in hygiene of pigs."

In 1918, Rankin left the Washington, D.C., apartment she'd shared with her mother, her widowed sister, and two little nieces. She went straight to the International Congress of Women in Zurich, Switzerland, where she shared a hotel room with Mary Church Terrell. While there, Rankin helped found the Women's International League for Peace and Freedom (WILPF), a group still active today.

Back in the United States, Rankin urged government officials to adopt WILPF policies. She was hired as a lobbyist for the National Consumers League in 1920. For four years, Rankin sought legislative support for child labor laws, mother and infant health care bills, a federally mandated minimum wage, and an eight-hour workday. Then she took time off to help her brother run (unsuccessfully) for the U.S. Senate.

Rankin took advantage of her brief unemployment to build a country house near Athens, Georgia. Although she maintained her Montana ranch, Rankin knew she would always find something to lobby for in Washington, D.C., and Georgia was closer than Montana. A carpenter's daughter, Rankin helped build a simple one-room house with a lean-to kitchen, surrounded by acres of peach and pecan trees. There was no indoor plumbing or electricity, even in 1972, when Rankin told a *New York Times* reporter, "Money shouldn't be a factor in our lives . . . I give all my money to the peace movement."

Rankin moved into her new home with a monthly income of $75 inherited from her father. That was a comfortable budget in 1924. From Georgia, Rankin lobbied for the WILPF and the Women's Peace Union, which worked to outlaw war in the United States. She cofounded the

It was women's work which was destroyed by war. Their work was raising human beings, and war destroyed human beings to protect profits and property.

—Jeannette Pickering Rankin

Georgia Peace Society, which worked to prove that wars were fought for profit, not principle. In 1929, she added the National Council for the Prevention of War (NCPW) to her lobbying list, work she pursued until 1938, even when the group's paychecks ran low.

During the presidential election in 1932, Rankin led a peace march. Starting in Washington, D.C., the marchers went to Chicago, where both the Democratic and Republican parties were holding their conventions. Young and old paraded with peace banners, urging the parties to work for peace. The parties didn't listen, but Rankin didn't give up. She simply changed tactics. Instead of pushing to outlaw war right away, Rankin lobbied for the 1935 Neutrality Act. The act outlawed the transport of war goods to warring nations. However, Rankin wasn't pleased that the act had to be renewed each year. Events in Europe troubled her. In 1939, Adolf Hitler sent German troops into Poland. Rankin wanted to do more than lobby for peace. She wanted to be in Congress again.

Almost 60 years old, Rankin hit the Montana campaign trail the way she had when she was 35. She spoke to people, in person and on the radio. She was concerned with global political unrest, but she also knew Americans needed help after the Great Depression. Her campaign slogan was: Prepare to the limit for defense; keep our men out of Europe. This plan would provide defense jobs at home without making America an "aggressor nation."

Rankin was reelected to the House of Representatives on November 5, 1940. She spent the first half of her term trying to prevent war. She introduced a resolution requiring a national election to find out if citizens wanted a war. Another proposal asked for congressional approval before troops could be deployed. But war came on December 8, 1941, one day after Pearl Harbor was bombed. Even though Rankin's vote against war again would do no good, "I voted against it because it was war," she said. This time, Rankin stood alone. She felt alone for the rest of her term. As the entire nation was swept into the war effort for "our boys over there," only Rankin worked to protect those who chose not to serve and those left with no income while family members served.

When her term was over in 1943, Rankin returned to Montana. "I always said that if we did go to war, I wouldn't run again because my friends and family would have to bear the brunt of criticism against me," Rankin said. The peace movement faded in the bright lights of the war effort, but Rankin's commitment to the cause did not. She traveled to India, to observe the nonviolent methods used by Mohandas Gandhi to achieve peaceful change. Over the next two decades, Rankin made six trips to India, as well as journeys to the Middle East, Asia, Africa, South America, Mexico, and Europe. Sometimes she attended conferences, like the 1949 World Pacifist Conference. Other times, she tried to travel among ordinary citizens, to experience life in their social and political climes. Though Rankin returned to her Georgia farm sometimes, she spent so much time abroad during these years that she "missed" being involved with the American civil rights movement of the 1950s and 1960s. But Rankin shared what she'd learned overseas with the press whenever she came home. In 1958, a young senator named John F. Kennedy wrote an article entitled "Three Women of Courage," calling Rankin one of the most fearless characters in American history.

> Y *ou can't settle disputes by shooting nice young men.*
>
> —Jeannette Pickering Rankin

Rankin finally brought her activism home again in 1967 when, at age 87, she started protesting U.S. involvement in the Vietnam War. Her studies of people around the world had turned Rankin into a "pure pacifist." She believed in immediate, universal disarmament. She would not compromise as the old Rankin had with war jobs for women or "preparing to the limit for defense." This Rankin told a reporter that women have "been worms. They let their sons go off to war because they're afraid their husbands will lose their jobs in industry if they protest."

So Rankin helped them protest. On January 15, 1968, Rankin led thousands who called themselves the Jeannette Rankin Brigade in an antiwar demonstration to the capital. Rankin picked up right where she had left off. She lobbied Congress for peace, to withdraw American troops and to listen to the American people. Suddenly, Rankin was famous again, as famous as she had been in 1917 when she was

Rankin voted against U.S. entry into both world wars. Near the end of her life, pacifist Rankin was asked if she'd change anything. She smiled. "This time, I'd be nastier."
(Montana Historical Society)

the "Lady from Montana." She spoke around the country. College students put up posters of her honest, wrinkled face. On June 11, 1970, the House of Representatives threw her a 90th birthday party. On February 12, 1972, the National Organization for Women (NOW) named Rankin the first member ever of its Susan B. Anthony Hall of Fame. In her acceptance speech to NOW, Rankin urged women not to forget that they could make a difference. "We could have peace in one year if women were organized," she said.

Jeannette Rankin died of heart failure on May 18, 1973, at the home her brother, Wellington, had left her in Carmel, California. Her ashes were scattered over the sea.

Chronology

JUNE 11, 1880	Jeannette Pickering Rankin born near Missoula, Montana
1902	graduates from University of Montana
1908	studies at New York School of Philanthropy
1910	joins Washington State woman suffrage campaign
1911	gives suffrage speech to Montana legislature
1912	is hired by National American Woman Suffrage Association (NAWSA)
1915	studies effects of woman suffrage in New Zealand
1916	is elected to U.S. House of Representatives
1917	votes against entering World War I
1918	introduces 19th Amendment to U.S. House; is defeated in reelection.
1924	moves to Georgia; begins congressional lobbyist work
1932	leads a peace march from Washington, D.C., to Chicago
1940	is reelected to House of Representatives
1941	votes against entry into World War II
1943	begins world travels

1967	protests U.S. involvement in the Vietnam War
1968	leads thousands in the Jeannette Rankin Brigade in Washington, D.C., antiwar demonstration
1970	House of Representatives honors Rankin's 90th birthday
1972	National Organization for Women (NOW) names Rankin first Susan B. Anthony Hall of Fame member
MAY 18, 1973	Jeannette Rankin dies of heart failure in Carmel, California

Further Reading

Brozan, Nadine. "Crusading Forerunner of Women's Lib," *New York Times*, January 24, 1972. A lively interview covering Rankin's past and present.

Davidson, Sue. *A Heart in Politics: Jeannette Rankin and Patsy T. Mink.* Seattle, Wash.: Seal Press, 1994. A detailed account of Rankin's life and work for young adult readers, with family and personal details. Contains some reconstructed dialogue.

Fox, Mary Virginia. *Pacifists: Adventures in Courage.* Chicago: Reilly and Lee Books, 1971. Rankin is one of 10 international pacifists featured in short profiles for young adult readers. Rankin's section focuses on her Congressional votes against war. Contains some reconstructed dialogue.

"House for Suffrage, 274 to 136," *New York Times*, January 11, 1918. A lengthy excerpt from Rankin's presentation of the Anthony Amendment to the U.S. Congress.

Morin, Isobel V. *Women of the U.S. Congress.* Minneapolis: Oliver Press, 1994. A short overview of Rankin's life for young adult readers.

Index

Boldface numbers indicate main topics. *Italic* numbers indicate illustrations. Page numbers followed by *c* indicate chronology.

141